In the name of Allah, the Magnificent, the Merciful

AL – FATEHA

&

ITS SIGNIFICANCE

SHAMIM A SIDDIQI

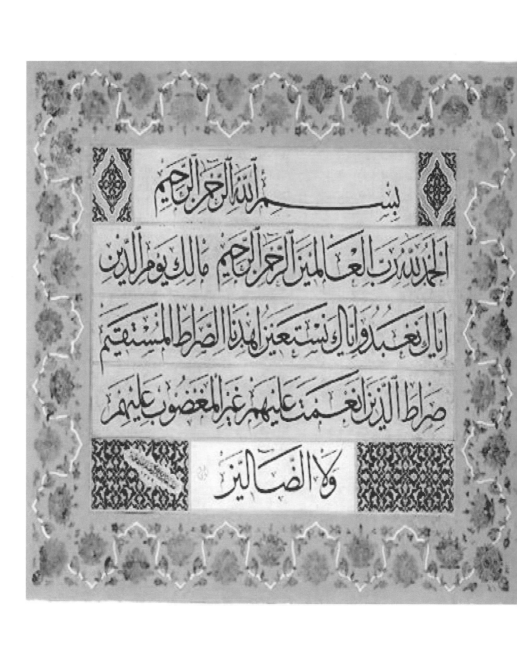

بِسْمِ اللّهِ الرَّحْمٰنِ الرَّحِيمِ

الْحَمْدُ لِلّهِ رَبِّ الْعَالَمِينَ الرَّحْمٰنِ الرَّحِيمِ مَالِكِ يَوْمِ الدِّينِ

إِيَّاكَ نَعْبُدُ وَإِيَّاكَ نَسْتَعِينُ اهْدِنَا الصِّرَاطَ الْمُسْتَقِيمَ

صِرَاطَ الَّذِينَ أَنْعَمْتَ عَلَيْهِمْ غَيْرِ الْمَغْضُوبِ عَلَيْهِمْ

وَلَا الضَّالِّينَ

The Forum Publication # IX

Published by   The Forum for Islamic Work
                      265 Flatbush Avenue,
                      Brooklyn, NY - 11355
                      Phone: 718 – 783 - 7708

Shamim A Siddiqi   AL- FATEHA & ITS SIGNIFICANCE
                      Address: 6 Plant Lane,
                               Westbury, NY- 11590
                      Phone: 516- 333- 4222

ISBN #   978-0-9819598-0-1

Price $6.00

Computer Work: Salman Mazhar,
                      Flushing, NY
                      516-884-3940

Printed   In the USA, Feb-March 2009
                      By: Sanatech Printing
                          37-28 56th Street
                          Woodside, NY-11377

D E D I C A T I O N

I

Dedicate

This book

To The Memory

Of

Late Baqar Khan Saheb

Of East Pakistan (Bangladesh)

&

My nephew

Late M. Qamar Alam Siddiqi

May Allah bless their soul

AMEEN!

v

In the name of Allah, the Beneficent, the Merciful

C O N T E N T S

FOREWORD

Surah al-Fatihah is a key to the understanding of the Qur'ān and epitomizes its entire message in seven verses. Muslim thinkers and sages have, in all times and climates, delved deeply into the meaning and significance of this sŭrah. The present study is an effort in the same direction by a contemporary student of the Qur'ān.

Not everybody's broth, exegesis is a difficult discipline, as it embraces a number of other disciplines from philology to lexicography and from philosophy to tradition and hermeneutics. In the past, our *mufassirin* (exegetes) pioneered exegetical literature in different domains. For example, if al-Zamakhshari's (d.1144) *al-Kashshaf [an Haqa'iq al-Tanzīl*, sparring its Mutazili slant, is rich in lexicographical and philological aspects, al-Qurtubi's (d.1272) *al-Jami[li Ahkam al-Qur'an* is distinguished for its deduction of laws, while al-Suyuti's (1505) *Tafsir al-Jalālayn, al-Durr al-Manthur fi al-Tafsir bi'l-Ma'thur* and *al-Itqan fi [ulum al-Qur'an* are studies in the sciences of the Qur'ān. In the traditional vein, we have ibn Kathir's (d.1337) *Tafsir al-Qur'an* explaining the Qur'an both through *tafsir bi'l-*Qur'an and *tafsir bi'l-Hadith*. In recent times we had Tantawi Jawhari's (d.1940) *al-Jawahir fi Tafsir al-Qur'an al-Karīm* interfacing religion with modern sciences.

In modern times we have Sayyid Qutb's *fi Zilal al-Qur'an* and Sayyid Mawdudi's *Tafhim al-Qur'an,* each exploring in his own way the relevance of the eternal word to the contemporary intellectual, moral and civilizational issues and challenges. Both respect tradition but at the same time venture into occasional lexicography, philology, reason, scholastics *(kalam)*. While *fi Zīlal al-Qur'an,* among other qualities, is a literary gem, *Tafhim al-Qur'an* brings to the study of the Qur'an a systemic approach essential in understanding Islam as a system embracing life. This variance in style and approaches towards understanding the Qur'ān in fact speaks of its versatility and inexhaustible potential.

This exegetical exuberance owes to the fact that from the early days of Islam people took the Qur'an seriously. It was not just another book but the Book meant for guidance shaping man's existential and spiritual potentials in a civilizational context. The development of the exegetical literature began the day when people started asking the Prophet *('alayhi as-salam)* questions on the meaning of the revelatory passages. It grew with the civilizational complexities faced by the Muslim Ummah in its effort to cope with them. Thus, it is not surprising that the corpus of our *tafsiri* literature is also reflective of different times and atmospherics, demonstrating human efforts not only to understand the meaning and message of the word of God, but also to discover its relevance to their own existence.

As opposed to the past, our today's challenges are far more complex. Not that humans have lost their clot of instincts but that there is a paradigmatic shift in the human situation — it is a technology shift which is influencing our behavior and attitudes against the backdrop of a continual change far more radical and deeper than in the previous times. Again, it is the planted secular consciousness promoted by Western civilization that not only defies religion but also clamps on humans what Comte calls "the renascent priesthood of Positivism." As Muslims, who believe in the revelatory response to life, we have to deal with modernity that demands throwing off normative values, language and epistemology. We have to place modernity's constituents like selfhood, individualism, rationality, freedom in the Islamic framework and then see how we can redeem these concepts from their ill-connotations and give them a healthy glow to the extent they reflect Islamic concepts and values.

Thus any new venture even if it is on a minor scale confined to explaining the contextual aspect of the *surah al-Fatihah*, as Br. Shamim Siddiqui has done, is praiseworthy. His selection of the *surah* is important for *al-Fatihah*, as Bukhari tells us, is considered as *umm al-kitab.* He has tried to explain its contents without abusing reason or emotions. Its prominent streak, however, remains traditional deriving from the Qur'an and *Sunnah*, with a

da[iyyah's compassion and zeal, to understand and share the message of the Qur'an. It constitutes a valuable edition to the rich literature on the exegesis of *al-Fatihah*.
May Allah the Exalted make it useful in changing human perceptions and attitudes. Amen.

Islamabad
Khurshid Ahmad*
December 30 2008

---

* Professor Khurshid Ahmad is the Senator in Pakistan and the Vice –President of J.I. Pakistan and the Member of its Shurah. He is prolific writer and the author of many books in Urdu and English. He is Editor of monthly Magazine Tarjumanul-Qur'an, Lahore

SPECIAL INTRODUCTORY NOTE

Br. Shamim Siddiqui's book on surah al-Fateha is a significant new addition to the existing literature on this essential introduction to the Qur'an.

Without a good understanding of al-Fateha, the Muslim cannot have correct understanding of the path ahead. As a sign of its importance, the Prophet Muhammad, peace be on him, made its recitation a requirement for each *rak'at* [unit] of prayer, be it *fard* or *Sunnah.*

Br. Shamim has spent his life in acquiring Islamic knowledge and in transmitting this knowledge to those who need it. He combines in himself the mindset of a pious Muslim and the width of understanding of a complex society such as America. He has discussed surah al-Fateha verse by verse and has explained both its contextual meaning and its relevance to our time and age.

This book should be a part of every library, Islamic and secular, which wants to provide correct orientation for understanding Islam.

It's an honor for me to write these few words about this small but sublime publication. May Allah reward Br. Shamim for this valuable endeavor.

Kaukab Siddique*
Baltimore, Maryland
December 15, 2008

Dr. Kaukab Siddique, the Founder President of Jamaat al-Muslimeen, is the Editor of New Trend Magazine on Internet, Prolific writer and author of many Books and papers and an eloquent speaker on his own merit. He has devoted his entire life in fighting against the sufferings of the oppressed in the USA and abroad.

Saying: "Thank You My Lord!"

The Qur'an's opening chapter Al-Fatiha is humanity's acknowledgment of God's unbound benevolence.

When someone gives us a gift or does a favor, however, small or trivial it may be, we instantly say "Thanks you!" If the favor is life-saving or life-long we keep on thanking the person for years."

Some who consciously or subconsciously become aware of God's bounties believe that a few empty rituals are all that they have to do to please God. The Muslims recite al-Fatiha - the opening chapter of the Qur'an – at least 17 times a day. Yet they are no exception. Islam, for them too has become a ritual to be dutifully observed without making any impact on their Muslim character and changing their life to that of an "Abd" (the one whose whole life is devoted to God).

Mr. Siddiqi has attempted to bring back the awareness of what believing in God means and how the opening chapter of the Qur'an perceives Divine : Human relationship.

The Qur'an reminds the humanity that God' fathomless mercy extends to all that is created and that as He is the most Loving, Most Gracious it should too behave in the most appropriate and beneficial manner.

The only way to thank God for His enormous gift of sustainable life is to show deep awareness of His Mercy every moment of one's life. Those who stay away from living the life of God-awareness are the most thankless creatures whether they do it in the name of freedom of thought, freedom of action or creating any other
philosophical paradigm.

May Allah accept Mr. Siddiqi's attempt to bring His Word to the humanity at large and create the real sense of what it means to be a Muslim among those who profess Islam.

Abu Iqbal *
October 18, 2008___

---

* Abu Iqbal is the pen name of Dr Omar Afzal. He is a scholar of Islamic Law [Fiqh] and Hadith in the USA/Canada. He is a prolific writer both in English and Urdu and has authored many books. A Da'ee Ilallah in his own merit, he constantly writes for different contemporary magazines and periodicals.

In the Name of Allah, the Beneficent, the Merciful

PREFACE

Alhamdulillah, I have completed, in my humble way, the commentary about Surah **Al-Fateha** as the **Preface to the Qur'an**, Allah's Book of Guidance for mankind on how to act, live and behave on earth in peace and harmony with others as His vicegerent with three strong physical urges: **[rest/sleep, hunger/thirst and sex]** and **a freewill**. Now it is up to the readers to opine how far I have been able to do justice with the theme and contents of this very precise, concise and all-comprehensive **Surah** (Chapter) of the Qur'an that carries the depth of an ocean in its meaning and concept.

This **Surah** has been under my keen evaluation and in-depth study for the last 30 years since the time I migrated to the USA in October 1976. The very next day of my arrival in New York, I was entrusted by my destiny to undertake this job by the opportunity extended to me by Allah (SWT). I must share the background with you.

I stayed with my nephew, the late Qamar Alam Siddiqi who came to the United States on an immigration visa two years ahead of me. The next day after my arrival in NY, in the evening hours, Qamar visited with me in the house of his friend Mohtaram Baqar Khan Saheb from East Pakistan (BD). At **Maghrib** time, he led the prayers at his home. When he started reciting **Surah Al-Fateha**, he started crying. It was a very astounding situation for me. I started thinking what made him cry so profoundly. I went on thinking and came to the realization that it was the depth of the meanings and the eloquent message of **Al-Fateha,** demanding devotion and commitment to Allah (SWT), and the overwhelming sense of responsibility that its contents invite one to shoulder that moved his heart, and he could not control the tears rolling down his cheeks. Baqar Bhai is no longer in this world. He died last year. I attended his **Salatul Janaza** in Jamaica Mosque and prayed for his **Maghfirah**.   He unconsciously introduced me to a very

passionately thoughtful situation that I could not forget for the whole of my life. He is a part of my regular **Du'a**. May Allah pardon his sins, if any, and place him in **Jannatul Firdaws. Amen!**
Since then, I have been constantly studying **Al-Fateha** and thinking about its various aspects time and again, and sharing my thoughts with friends and others in the Qur'anic study sessions. Last year, when he died, I decided to write down what I have been thinking about **Al-Fateha** and dedicate it to his memory and to that of Qamar Mian. Both are no longer in this world. May Allah bless the souls of both and grace them with His best rewards. **Amen!**

I took up this task in mid April 2008 and, by the grace of Allah, completed it in the third week of July 08. I pray to Almighty Allah to accept it as my humble contribution towards the resurrection of the Muslim **Ummah** as no other cause is greater and more sacred than its revival at this juncture when Muslims have been rendered into the most degraded and downtrodden people (**Millah**) of the world..

Allah (SWT) entrusted the mission of establishing His authority and His **Deen Al-Islam** in this world to **Prophet Muhammad (S)**. He (S) first established it in the body politics of the Arabian Peninsula and then his (S) faithful followers carried out his (S) mission to every nook and corner of the entire world known to human society at that time. It was all done within the first hundred years of the advent of Islam, from the boarders of China to the Atlantic coast, from Yemen to Central Europe and up to the Philippines in the Far East. The **Qur'an** was the motivational force, with <u>**its paramount message of justice, peace and equality for the entire humanity,**</u> behind this whirlwind success in such a short time. They introduced to the world **afresh** the concept of **Tawheed** (Monotheism) and the accountability of man, in **Akhirah** (**The Hereafter**) after death, for all his actions and deeds on earth. They followed the **life pattern of Rasulullah (S) as their model.** Let us first understand who Allah is and what He is doing for us?

WHO IS ALLAH?

Al-Fateha defines who Allah, or our God, is at the very outset

as the Preface of the Qur'an.

Allah is One, who is 'Al-Rahman, Al-Raheem, the Creator and the Sustainer of this cosmos and is wonderfully sustaining the human species along with it. We are enjoying His countless bounties, with the constant feeling that they are not "<u>free</u>." We all are accountable to Him for the way we utilize and enjoy His endless bounties on earth. One Day [known to Him alone] all will be present in His Supreme Court, and every human being will be accountable for the way he/she used His favors and bounties on earth: the way He ordained through His appointed Messengers or the way he/she used as per his/her freewill. The culminating point of this life will commence when each human being will be either entering into Jannah (paradise) if he/she lived, acted and behaved on earth the way He ordained, or be thrown in the ditch of Hellfire, if the case would be the reverse.

This is the essence of man's temporary stay on earth, irrespective of what faith he/she holds, provided he/she is human, not a beast. <u>Al-Fateha</u> brilliantly puts this entire basic phenomenon of man's living condition on earth in three simple words and phrases, expressing his/her inner gratitude to the Lord of this universe.

* Alhamdulillahey Rabbil 'A'lameen   [All praise is for the Sustainer of this cosmos]

* Al-Rahman Al-Raheem   [He is the Beneficent, the Merciful]

* Ma'likey Yawmiddeen [His authority will be Supreme on the Day of Judgment]

It connotes that the One Who is providing all the necessities of one's existence on earth, looking after all human needs and urgencies, protecting us form all the eventualities around us, is none but the Sustainer of this universe. His infinite mercy controls all the phases of our life from when we are in the wombs of our mothers till we are buried in graves, and continues till the human life completes its journey on the Day of Judgment when our fate will be finally decided for good. It is He Who is our Sustainer all through. Only He can be our "Rabb," the Creator and Sustainer, the Lord of this universe. With the intensity of this realization the human's heart is filled with a profound sense of gratitude to His Lord and feels all grateful to Him and His magnanimities all through his/her journey to the eternity.

It is essential that this deep rooted human acknowledgment must be shared with our fellow citizens, the Judeo - Christian - pagan world, and they should be invited to think about it deeply to realize what the Sustainer of this cosmos is doing for us and how we are behaving with His countless favors and bounties that we all are enjoying day in and day out. Should we not feel obliged and be obedient to Him in return? This realization should be shared with every individual being with love, care and concern at a person to person level by every Muslim and Muslimah occupying this abode of man, invoking the most natural process of Dawah Ilallah, calling the people to the fold of their Creator and Sustainer.

It is the onerous task of every Muslim on earth to present this all-surmounting love of God for humanity that He is the Sustainer of all humans. Yet how are they behaving with the Guidance that He has ordained for them to live on earth in peace and harmony? In fact, He is the Sustainer of all, the entire humanity. Muslims are no exception to it. It is incumbent upon Muslims to organize a whirlwind campaign around the world, especially in the West that: GOD IS FOR ALL AND FOR EVERYONE - Our God is extremely kind and merciful beyond our imagination and, as such, we humans must rush to the Lord of this Universe, with repentance over our past behavior. He loves to pardon His "slaves" who repent and accept Him as their Lord, then live a life of obedience to Him in every walk of life. This message of HOPE is eternal from Him. Any time humans can turn their face to Him. He is ever ready to embrace them. <u>One who accepts Him as his Lord, he declares solemnly</u>:

* "My God is the only One who takes care of me and my total physical and moral needs. He is <u>Rabbil 'Alameen,</u> the Sustainer of all worlds;

* "Feeling His favors and bounties all around, my heart is filled with fathomless gratitude (Shukr) and I eloquently confess that the Praise is only for the Lord of the universe. My entire existence depends on this realization. I express this confession by declaring: '<u>Alhamdulillahey Rabbil 'A'lameen.</u>'"

* This brings him to the most logical questions about his existence on earth: How does he behave on earth? How does he use His bounties in the service of the Lord: as He commands, or does he behave recklessly against His will and the system He has ordained for humans to follow and, thus, creating only Fasad (transgression) on His earth?

* This self-realization would convince him to lead a responsible life, feeling always accountable to his Lord on the Day of Judgment after death.

* Making him conscious of the fact that his entering into heaven, the place of eternal bliss, or going to hell, the place of eternal torment, <u>depends</u> on the attitude of life that he adopts on earth through exercising his own free will. <u>The choice is his/hers.</u>

* Thus, the scenario of Accountability on the Last Day of Judgment will incline every individual human being to turn his face to his Creator and Sustainer, repent and seek His pardon and commit to be obedient to Him always - the surest way to have salvation in the life Hereafter.

* It would be the simplest way to present Islam (Peace) to the people of the world, giving them every opportunity to think

about their position on earth and provide them with complete freedom to choose "Islam" as the "System of life" to make their worldly life easy and balanced. It is the only way to fill both our worlds with countless blessings and benedictions before and after death.

NO GENDER DIFFERENCE WITH ALLAH:

Guidance that comes from the Creator and Sustainer does not distinguish between male and female. The addressees are humans, the progenies of Adam. With Allah (SWT) it is deeds that count, not the gender, as spelled out in <u>Verse # 97 of Surah # 16, Al-Nahl:</u>

مَنْ عَمِلَ صَالِحًا مِنْ ذَكَرٍ أَوْ أُنْثَىٰ وَهُوَ مُؤْمِنٌ فَلَنُحْيِيَنَّهُ حَيَاةً طَيِّبَةً ۖ وَلَنَجْزِيَنَّهُمْ أَجْرَهُمْ بِأَحْسَنِ مَا كَانُوا يَعْمَلُونَ

"Whosoever does right, whether male or female and is a believer (Mu'min) him verily We shall quicken with good life, and We shall pay them recompense in proportion to the best of what they used to do."

The aforesaid task to share the paramount message of Islam with the secular world lies evenly on the shoulders of both genders of the Muslim Ummah in their respective spheres. As such, the addressees of this book, as in the Qur'an are both Muslim men and Muslim women, irrespective of whether it is spelled out in the context or not. The revival of the Muslim Ummah will not be possible if this responsibility is not cherished equally by our sisters.

AL-FATEHA MAKES THE QUR'AN EASY TO UNDERSTAND:

The genesis of the Deen Al-Islam can be summarized as follows:

1. God created this universe and what it contains for man and harnessed it for him to use for the satisfaction of his needs and urges according to his free will;

2. Man, therefore, always begs for Guidance as his greatest need as to how to live, act and behave on this earth in order to fill the earth with justice and live in peace and harmony with his species;

3. Guidance comes from the Lord of this cosmos, our Creator and Sustainer through His commitment to Adam when He asked him to go down to earth as His Vicegerent. Our Sustainer keeps the account of each individual human being, how he is behaving with respect to the Guidance and using His bounties for which he will be held accountable on the Day of Judgment. Accordingly, each human being will be rewarded or punished.

<u>Al-Fateha</u> marvelously covers all these comprehensive aspects of human life on earth in a couple of brief but very meaningful, concise and precise sentences. **It presents the Qur'an in miniature**. The reader will judge how far I have been successful in presenting the essence of the Qur'an in terms of <u>Al-Fateha</u> in the following pages to enable Muslim brothers and sisters around the world to uphold the message of the Qur'an in a nut shell and <u>share it with "suffering" humanity, both the affluent and the have-nots</u> and be the effective Da'ee Ilallah (caller to the path of Allah) in the context of the modern world.

I am extremely grateful to "My God" for inspiring me to undertake this most difficult task of my life to write "some words" about His most miraculous verses in my humble way. I expect my "AJR" (reward) only from Him and you know He is extraordinarily magnanimous in showering His blessings on His "ABD" (slave) when <u>he totally surrenders to Him with all</u>

humility and seeks help only from Him ["Iyyaka Na'budu wa Iyyaka Nasta'een"].

AL-DU'A (supplication) _ - All my praise is for Allah (SWT) alone –"Al-Hamdu Lillahi Rabbil 'Alameen", Who gave me Tawfeeq (favor) to evaluate the Al-Fatiha in depth and find out only the essence of His obedient slave on earth – a Muslim. I am sure that on the Day of Judgment my most humble work will become my most eloquent witness in His Mighty Court, "begging" for my Maghfirah (forgiveness) and that of my parents and the benevolent teachers whose prayers always guide my destiny to this glorious end. Amen!

Shamim A Siddiqi
WWW.dawahinamericas.com
Ramadan 8, 1429 H/ September 9, 2008

ACKNOWLEDGMENT

* In this domain my first and the foremost acknowledgment must go to the infinite Rahmah of my Benevolent and Merciful Creator and Sustainer Who inspired my innerself to write this short Commentary about the <u>"Preface to the Qur'an"</u> with a vision to present Islam in its correct perspective and get the fate of Muslim Ummah revived in its wake. May Allah accept my humble efforts and transform my vision into a reality!

* At the same time, I must acknowledge the love and care of my late parents, Late Sheikh Hafizullah and Bibi Rukayyah and my beloved teachers, especially my elder brother Dr Jamil A Siddiqi whose prayers and guidance always help me to follow the path of righteousness and speak only truth. May Allah bless each of them immensely, pardon their sins, if any, and place them in Jannatul Firdaus!

* In this process, the most positive contribution was made by my beloved Brother Dr. Erdugan Gurman and his well educated wife in editing the draft twice and rendering valuable suggestions towards the improvement of the Message of Al-Fateha in an effective manner. May Allah bless both of them immensely!

* Equally, I must appreciate the valuable services rendered by my third son Ejaz A Siddiqi and my grandson [Nawasa] Salman Mazhar for helping me all through for all the computer jobs not once but many a times and in transforming the book into the camera ready face for printing. My second son Talha Nadeem Siddiqi did great job in inserting the Qur'anic Verses and their English translation at appropriate places in the text of this book. May Allah bless each of them and give Barakah in their "Ilm" and expertise in their profession. He also beautifully designed the cover of the book.

May Allah bless all the brothers and sisters immensely who helped in getting this book published in any form, kind or shape. May Allah reward them in both the worlds in abundance!

In the name of Allah, the Magnificent, the Merciful

AL-FATEHA & ITS SIGNIFICANCE

INTRODUCTION:

Al-Qur'an is the final Book of Guidance from our Creator and Sustainer, the Lord of this cosmos, to guide the affairs of His servants [human beings] on how to live act and behave on this earth. It was revealed to **Prophet Muhammad (S)** 1400 years ago and it is totally intact in its original form, language and contents. It guided Rasulullah (S) during 23 years of his (S) constant efforts to establish the Deen of Allah on this earth, and to inculcate a God-fearing, trustworthy character in the people who responded to his (S) call of **Dawah Ilallah** (Inviting to the fold of Allah), deliver justice and peace to human society by providing a sound and well-balanced socio-economic-political system and leaving behind the truthful and praiseworthy model of himself (S) for humanity to follow till eternity.

Surah Al-Fateha is the opening Chapter of this Glorious Book, **Al-Qur'an**. This Surah was revealed in the very early stage of the Makkan period. It is in the form of a **Du'a** (supplication) reminding every Muslim and Muslimah that if he/she wants to benefit from the **Qur'an** he/she must supplicate to Allah (SWT) very humbly in the manner that is called upon in its contents. It teaches us how to implore to Allah, and the Teacher is God Himself. It ensures the acceptance of the prayers very realistically as the Master is teaching us how to beg and seek His help and guidance. It is the introduction to the **Qur'an**, telling us what it contains and to what spiritual heights it is inviting human beings to attain while on earth. **It creates a direct link between God and His servants**. It is a spontaneous expression of man's sense of gratitude to his Creator and Sustainer for what he possesses and what He has done or is doing for him on a continuous basis to sustain the human's life on earth. These realizations automatically incline man to surrender to

His authority in total submission and beg for all of his needs and urgencies only from Him. **It is, therefore, essential that we must try to elaborate on all these enlightening essential aspects of this Surah meticulously so that the followers of the Deen of Allah develop a personal contact earnestly with the Lord of the universe and prepare themselves to surrender to His will totally while living on His earth and seeking only His pleasure in every walk of life.**

In fact, this **Surah** cements the relation of the servant of Allah with his Master right at the very outset of the **Salah** (Daily Prayers), creating a personal contact between man and God, totally surrendering himself to the will of His Sustainer, and seeking help and guidance only from Him. It fixes the **submissive tone of the Salah**, cuts the worshipper off from the rest of the world while in prayers, leaving him completely absorbed in Him in rapt adoration. Only such **Salah** becomes the source of inspiration. It helps in consolidating his personality for the pleasure of Allah, creating a direct relation with the Creator and Sustainer. It fills his heart and mind with total devotion, preparing him for sacrificing all that he possesses towards establishing His authority on self, family and in the society in which he lives. This state of mind and heart brings him to the climax of "servitude" to his Master. **Only such men or women will be the "salt of the sea and lamp of the mountain." <u>Surah Al-Fateha is, thus, an important instrument for a Muslim in becoming His praiseworthy and loveable " 'Abd" (slave), and there lies its significance in paving the way towards the man's attainment of communion with his Creator and Sustainer, in reaching that requisite point of "zenith" of a Mu'min [Ref: Verse # 27 -30 of Surah # 89, Al-Fajr]</u>**

Realizing this significance throughout my life, cautiously and consciously, I developed the conviction that one who wants to perfect his **Salah** and live on earth as Allah's most humble servant, must cement his relations with his Lord, he must understand **Surah Al-Fateha** with all its comprehensiveness and conceptual connotations that it inherits in its scope and in the forefront as the

Preface of the Qur'an. *It quenches the human thirst to attain the highest order of spiritual perfection to be declared by Allah on the Day of Judgment:* "Ya Ayyatuhun-Al-Nafsul-Mutmainnah": *"O the Contented soul!*

يَا أَيَّتُهَا النَّفْسُ الْمُطْمَئِنَّةُ
ارْجِعِي إِلَى رَبِّكِ رَاضِيَة مَّرْضِيَّة
فَادْخُلِي فِي عِبَادِي
وَادْخُلِي جَنَّتِي

"O the Contented soul!
Return unto your Lord, content in His good pleasure!
Enter you amongst My bondsmen.
Enter you (in) My Jannah".

[Qur'an, Surah Al-Fajr: 89: 27 - 30]

This would be the best scenario for a Muslim on the Day of Judgment to envision and cherish, to be welcomed like that by the Supreme Lord of the cosmos for totally serving Him on earth. It would be the perfection of the human being's evolutionary process, starting from an embryo, to attain the supreme and the most accomplished position and to become ultimately His "'Abd" (slave) for whom the Creator and Sustainer created this universe and sustaining it out of His infinite Rahmah. It would be the most phenomenal success of his life-long endeavors on earth as a Muslim and a Da'ee Ilallah. It would be possible for him to attain this coveted position if he lives and dies under the constant image of Surah Al-Fateha and struggles to be its living embodiment on earth in thoughts and actions.

May Allah give immense Tawfeeq to each and every Muslim and Muslimah to be worthy of this scenario when facing his/her Lord on the Day of Judgment with the only assets of

Iman (total belief) and 'Amal-us-Salih (good deeds) that he/she had collected and treasured on earth as the Provision for Akhirah. Amen!

<u>**1, IMPORTANCE OF AL-FATEHA:**</u>

* **Surah Al-Fateha** is recited at least seventeen times daily by every Muslim in his obligatory **Salah**. It consists of seven verses including **Bismillah Al-Rahman Al-Raheem, as the opening first verse.** They are the <u>**"Sab'an min Al-mathani"**</u> **[seven oft-repeated (verses)], [Ref: Qur'an, Surah Al-Hijr, 15: 87].**

وَلَقَدْ آتَيْنَاكَ سَبْعًا مِنَ الْمَثَانِي وَالْقُرْآنَ الْعَظِيمَ

The beauty of these verses becomes more fascinating when one understands the meanings and concept in depth; and he will love it more. And the more he loves it, the more he will recite it with deep devotion and rapt adoration of Allah's grace, mercy and bounties that He is showering on His slave ['**Abd**.]. Thus, the closer he will feel to his Lord.

* The **Salah** (prayer) is the most important **'Ibadah** (worship) of a Muslim. He offers it at least five times a day on a regular basis. His **Salah** becomes invalid if he does not recite **Al-Fateha** in every **Rak'ah**. Rather, every **Rak'ah** starts by reciting **Al-Fateha** at the very outset of the prayers after making intention for the **Salah**, as Abu Hurairah (RA) narrates in a **Hadith** from Rasulullah (S):

<u>**"La Salata leman lam yaqrau Al-Fateha"**</u> [Translation: The **Salah** becomes invalid for the person who does not recite **Al-Fateha** in it]

* **Baihaqi**, in his book **Sha'bul Iman**, through correct authentication quotes that Rasulullah (S) said, <u>**"Al-Fateha is a cure for all diseases,"**</u> as quoted in **"Ma'riful Qur'an"** by Maulana Mufti Shafi Sahib at page 73 of his **Tafseer**.

* Abu Sayeed Khudri, [his complete name was **Saa'd bin Malik**

Khudri Ansari (RA)], the famous companion of Rasulullah (S), was once leading a platoon of 30 **Sahabah [Companions of Rasulullah (S)]**. He and his companions were short of food. They approached a village on the way but the people of the village refused to entertain them. They stayed outside the village. Meanwhile, the tribal chief was bitten by a scorpion. He was in great pain. Village people came to the companions of the Prophet (S) and asked for help to get their chief cured. Abu Sayeed Khudri (RA) said, "I will do it but I will charge 30 goats in lieu of that." They agreed. He went to the village, recited **Al-Fateha** and "blew" it on the tribal chief and then blew on the wound. He was cured. The village people gave him 30 goats as promised.

Sayeed Khudri (RA) said to his companions, "We will not eat the meat till we consult Rasulullah (S)." They reached Madinah and narrated the whole story to Rasulullah (S). Rasulullah (S) smiled and justified this bargain, and to make it easy for them asked to have his (S) share too. This establishes the miraculous effect of **Surah Al-Fateha**. **[As narrated by Bukhari]**

2. <u>THE PREFACE TO THE QUR'AN:</u>

Surah Al-Fateha carries different names:

"Fatihatul Kitab" [The opening chapter of the book]; It is also called "Ummul Kitab"; and "Kafiyah."

<u>It is the Preface to the Qur'an:</u> A "Preface" is an introduction to a book by the author, briefly elucidating what the book contains, what are its main themes, scope or subjects that are dealt with in it. **Al-Fateha** tells about the main themes of the Qur'an, the paramount fundamentals of Deen that it elaborates – * **Tawheed**, * **Prophethood and * Accountability in Akhirah.** Maulana Amin Ahsan Islahi (RA) in his monumental **Tafseer <u>"Tadabbur-al-Qur'an"</u>** has elaborated on three reasons for which **Al-Fateha** is to be treated as the Preface to the Qur'an.

1. It tells the starting point of **Deen**, pinpointing what can be the beginning of the worship of Allah and what are its motivations. It tells about the signs of Allah's favors, blessings and the vast arrangement that He has made for the nourishment and maintenance of our species and this universe with extreme regularity and extra-ordinary accuracy. The entire system of this cosmos, including the abode of man, is under constant operation day and night, round the clock, inclining humans to express their gratitude [thanks], motivating them to worship their Sustainer alone, inspiring them to seek help only from Him, imploring Him for guidance on how to live on earth, and begging Him to keep them on the straight path of righteousness. This is the natural process of the development of the human inclination towards seeking guidance from the Creator and Sustainer and towards fulfilling that fundamental urge of man to be always following the path of righteousness. For meeting this basic need of man, Allah (SWT), in His infinite mercy, appointed His Messengers on earth over the centuries in a continuous process. This **Surah** presents this entire scenario in a very precise and concise manner, thereby rendering it to be the **Preface of the Qur'an.**

2. The contents or the subject matter of the **Qur'an** can be categorized into three themes:

*<u>**Tawheed (Monotheism)**</u>;

* <u>**Accountability in Akhirah (The Day of Judgment)**</u>;

*<u>**Risalah (Prophethood).**</u>

The first two verses of **Al-Fateha** [<u>**"Alhamdulillahey Rabbil 'Alameen**</u>; <u>**Al-Rahman Al-Raheem"**</u>] present "Allah" as the Master and the Sustainer of the entire cosmos and, as such, the center of all praise and gratitude, worthy of worship – thus establishing and perfecting the concept of **Tawheed** directly in our hearts and minds.

The third verse: <u>**"Ma'likey Yawmiddeen"**</u> describes the continuation of His mercy to the Day of Judgment where He will be the sole Master.

The fourth verse: **"Iyyaka Na'budu wa Iyyaka Nasta'een"** represents the state of total surrender of man to his/her Creator and Sustainer, fulfilling the most important characteristic of **Tawheed**.

The fifth verse: **"Ihdina-al-Sirat-al-Mustaqeem"** is in the form of a prayer of man showing that we totally depend for guidance on His appointed Messengers **[establishing the Need of Prophet].** [Rest is the qualification of this prayer of the Mumin]

Thus, this small **Surah** of seven simple verses emerges as the **Preface to the Qur'an**, by meeting the basic needs of man for guidance: **why, from where and how does it come? The explanation and elaboration of these themes covers the entire spectrum of the Qur'an.**

3. The **Surah** depicts the inner thirst of our self for guidance, leading to the revelation of the **Qur'an**. Allah showed the straight path to the Jews and **Nasara** (Christians), but neither could they keep themselves upright along the path of righteousness nor could they call humanity to that path. Rather, they lost the guidance sent to them and left the humanity to grapple with the gloom and darkness of ignorance all around. This **Surah** is the deep expression of that urge to come out of that darkness and through His kindness humanity got the light from the blessings of the Qur'an. Only the **Du'a** (supplication) in the form of **Al- Fateha** could keep us steadfast on the path of righteousness, guide us to seek the solution to the problems in our life on earth and obtain salvation in the life Hereafter.

This concept of Al-Fateha as the Preface to the Qur'an will further crystallize when we will study it in detail verse by verse, Insha Allah.

CHAPTER - 1

A L- F A T E H A – MEANINGS & CONCEPT

I, <u>Verse # 1</u> – "Bismillah-al-Rahman-al-Raheem":

بِسْمِ اللَّهِ الرَّحْمَـٰنِ الرَّحِيمِ

<u>Translation</u>: In the name of Allah, the most Gracious, the most Merciful.

- Many scholars are of the opinion that **"Bismillah"** is a part of **Al-Fateha** whereas many others think otherwise. However, the qualification of **"Sab'an Min Al-Mathani"** [Ref: Surah Hijr, 15: 87] is only applicable to the seven verses of **Al-Fateha**. If one takes out the **"Bismillah-Al-Rahman-Al-Raheem"** not as its part, it would leave only six verses in **Al-Fatiha**. Hence, it would not qualify to be taken as the **"seven off-repeated verses"** of the Qur'an. I have, therefore, taken **"Bismillah-al-Rahman-al-Raheem"** as an integral part of **Al-Fateha** as a majority of Muslim scholars have opined. It gives **Al-Fateha** the requisite seven verses for its qualification to be called as **"Sab'an Min Al-Mathani.'** In the **Qur'an, "Bismillah-al-Rahman-al-Raheem"** also is the part of **Verse 30** in **Surah # 27, Al-Naml:**

إِنَّهُ مِنْ سُلَيْمَانَ وَإِنَّهُ بِسْمِ اللَّهِ الرَّحْمَـٰنِ الرَّحِيمِ

"...Lo! It (the letter) is from Solomon, and lo! It is: In the name of Allah, Most Gracious, and Most Merciful ("Bismillah-al-Rahman-al-Raheem").

- This **verse** constitutes the proper name of **"ALLAH"** and His two most important attributes: <u>*Al-Rahman</u> and <u>*Al-Raheem. That is also known as "Ismul Azam,"</u> the Great Names of Allah.

- Allah: The word "Allah" was arrived at after adding in the beginning **"Alif Lam,"** the symbols of the proper noun, on "ILAH." This word **"Allah"** is particularly used   for the Creator of humans, the cosmos, and what it contains. **Arabs** during **Jahiliyah** (Ignorance) understood it in the same context. In spite of this fact, Arabs were idolaters but they never gave this name to any of their idols. They used to confess that the Creator of the earth, skies and all species is Allah alone and none was equal to Him. He created the sun and the moon and harnessed them for human use. He is the only One who is sending rain and providing **Rizq** (provision) to us. The idols whom Arabs were worshipping were, however, taken only the means of intercession to Allah and as they, as per the pagan's understanding or estimation, were "closer" to Him. The Qur'an has totally nullified these concepts of Arab **Jahiliyah** (Ignorance) in **Verse # 3 of Al-Zumar & Verses # 61 - 63 of Al-Ankabut.[Ref: Tadabbur-al-Qur'an, Page 5**

أَلَا لِلَّهِ الدِّينُ الْخَالِصُ ۚ وَالَّذِينَ اتَّخَذُوا مِنْ دُونِهِ أَوْلِيَاءَ مَا نَعْبُدُهُمْ إِلَّا لِيُقَرِّبُونَا إِلَى
اللَّهِ زُلْفَىٰ إِنَّ اللَّهَ يَحْكُمُ بَيْنَهُمْ فِي مَا هُمْ فِيهِ يَخْتَلِفُونَ ۗ إِنَّ اللَّهَ لَا يَهْدِي مَنْ هُوَ كَاذِبٌ كَفَّارٌ

"Surely pure Deen is for Allah only. And those who choose protecting friends beside Him (say): We worship them only that they may bring us nearer to Allah. Lo! Allah will judge between them concerning that where they differ. Lo! Allah guides not him who is liar and ingrate."

[Qur'an, Surah Al-Zumar 39: 3]

وَلَئِنْ سَأَلْتَهُمْ مَنْ نَزَّلَ مِنَ السَّمَاءِ مَاءً فَأَحْيَا بِهِ الْأَرْضَ مِنْ بَعْدِ مَوْتِهَا لَيَقُولُنَّ اللَّهُ ۚ قُلِ الْحَمْدُ لِلَّهِ ۚ بَلْ أَكْثَرُهُمْ لَا يَعْقِلُونَ

* And if you were to ask them: Who causes water to come down from the sky, and therewith revives the earth after its

death? They verily would say: Allah. Say: Praise be to Allah!
But most of them have no sense."

[Qur'an, Surah Al-Ankabut 29: 63]

- AL-RAHMAN:

فَرَجَعَ مُوسَىٰ إِلَىٰ قَوْمِهِ غَضْبَانَ أَسِف

Then Moses went back unto his folk, angry and sad.

(Qur'an, Surah Taha, 20:86)

وَلَمَّا رَجَعَ مُوسَىٰ إِلَىٰ قَوْمِهِ غَضْبَانَ أَسِقًا

and when Moses returned unto his people, angry and grieved

(Qur'an, Surah Al-A'raf, 7:150)

Al-RAHMAN: It is in the Arabic grammatical measurement of **"Fa'alan":** as the word **"Ghadaban"** - manifestation of extreme anger – bursting with anger. **[Ref: Taha -20: 86 and Al-A'raf 7: 150 (as quoted above)]** So, **Al-Rahman** means manifestation and exuberance of extreme kindness; full of unrestrained enthusiasm towards manifesting His kindness.

Allah is **"Al- Rahman"** - Most Kind and Merciful and out of the manifestation of His extreme kindness He created this universe and what it contains **for mankind** but equally at the same time He is **"Al- Raheem."** So, He is maintaining and sustaining the universe for the **continuation of the human species**. Let us examine the characteristic of **Al-Raheem**.

- Al-Raheem: It is in the Arabic grammatical measurement of **"Taf'eel"** as **"Kareem,"** carrying the concept of **permanency, eternity:** confirming and assuring the continuity of Allah's Kindness for His creation for good towards maintaining and sustaining all that He created in this cosmos out of His attribute of **Al-Rahman**.

To have an idea of how much Allah is **Al- Rahman and Al-**

Raheem in sustaining us, just take a piece of bread in your hand; don't eat it, hold it in your hand in front of your mouth and think what innumerable and countless forces Allah has used from heaven down to earth in producing and providing that piece of bread for keeping us alive on this earth. If you think over His favors, bounties and benedictions, you will never be able to count them.   **Allah** is providing us all because He is **Al-Rahman** and at the same time **Al-Raheem,** too. That fills our heart with the extreme sense of gratitude (**Shukr**) to Him, and the grateful heart cries: <u>**"Al-Hamdu Lillahi Rabbil 'Alameen"**</u> - **All praise and thanks are only for Allah who is the Sustainer of this cosmos.**

This kindness of Allah continues till **Qiyamah** (The Day of Judgment) which is the culminating point of His **Rahmah** that *He showers upon all His creatures while on earth but will be special on the Day of Judgment for those of His "servants" ["Abd"] who followed Him on earth by their freewill.*

II. <u>VERRSE # 2: "Al-Hamdu Lillahi Rabbil 'Alameen"</u>:

الْحَمْدُ لِلَّهِ رَبِّ الْعَالَمِينَ

Translation: <u>All praise is for Allah who is the Rabb, the Sustainer of all worlds, the entire cosmos and what it contains, including all the living species.</u>

Allah is **"Rabb,"** the Sustainer and the Cherisher of all that exists in this universe. The way He sustains it is marvelous, elaborate and meticulously planned and executed to its minutest details. Just take the example of the human species and observe the extraordinary planning that Allah makes from the beginning to the end.
Allah created first the frame of Adam (AS), the father of man, from clay, a mixture of mud and water and fashioned it to a perfect

shape [**Fi Ahsane Taqweem,** the best stature]. Then He asked the angels, the working Agents of His Empire to bow down before him to establish his superiority over the angels due to **"Ilm"- the knowledge of all things** - that He imparted to Adam earlier. He then kept him (Adam) in **Jannah** (Paradise) till the world, the "temporary" abode of man, became habitable for him by putting/arranging all that man would need on earth till the doomsday. During this process, both the Devilish forces and Adam were tested by Allah. **Iblees** (Shaitan) proved to be ungrateful due to arrogance and Adam became grateful to Allah through his repentance. The embodiments of these two characters – man, the grateful and the devil, the ungrateful – which were and are "enemy" to each other descended to live on earth through the process of procreation to prove who is worthy of an eternal life in heaven and who encounters eternal condemnation in Hellfire by exercising the free will that Allah gave to human species.

Now let us see the process or procreation of man on earth, how minutely Allah describes it in **Verse # 5 of Surah # 22, Al- Hajj :**

يَا أَيُّهَا النَّاسُ إِنْ كُنْتُمْ فِي رَيْبٍ مِنَ الْبَعْثِ فَإِنَّا خَلَقْنَاكُمْ مِنْ تُرَابٍ ثُمَّ مِنْ نُطْفَةٍ ثُمَّ مِنْ عَلَقَةٍ ثُمَّ مِنْ مُضْغَةٍ مُخَلَّقَةٍ وَغَيْرِ مُخَلَّقَةٍ لِنُبَيِّنَ لَكُمْ ۚ وَنُقِرُّ فِي الْأَرْحَامِ مَا نَشَاءُ إِلَىٰ أَجَلٍ مُسَمًّى ثُمَّ نُخْرِجُكُمْ طِفْلًا ثُمَّ لِتَبْلُغُوا أَشُدَّكُمْ ۖ وَمِنْكُمْ مَنْ يُتَوَفَّىٰ وَمِنْكُمْ مَنْ يُرَدُّ إِلَىٰ أَرْذَلِ الْعُمُرِ لِكَيْلَا يَعْلَمَ مِنْ بَعْدِ عِلْمٍ شَيْئًا

"O mankind! If you are in doubt concerning the Resurrection, [then think]! We have created you from dust, then from a drop of seed, then from a clot, then from a little lump of flesh shapely and shapeless, that we make (it) clear for you. And We cause what We will to remain in the wombs for an appointed time, and afterward We bring you forth as infants, then (give you growth) that you attain your full strength. And among you there is he who dies (young), and among you there is he who

is brought back to the most abject time of life, so that, after knowledge, he knows naught..."

Allah (SWT) has given this vivid description of man's process of creation and growth in stages and evolutionary process at many other places in the Qur'an:

وَلَقَدْ خَلَقْنَا الْإِنْسَانَ مِنْ سُلَالَةٍ مِنْ طِينٍ
ثُمَّ جَعَلْنَاهُ نُطْفَةً فِي قَرَارٍ مَكِينٍ
ثُمَّ خَلَقْنَا النُّطْفَةَ عَلَقَةً فَخَلَقْنَا الْعَلَقَةَ مُضْغَةً فَخَلَقْنَا الْمُضْغَةَ عِظَامًا فَكَسَوْنَا
الْعِظَامَ لَحْمًا ثُمَّ أَنْشَأْنَاهُ خَلْقًا آخَرَ ۚ فَتَبَارَكَ اللَّهُ أَحْسَنُ الْخَالِقِينَ

"Verily We created man from a product of wet earth; Then placed him as a drop (of seed) in a safe lodging; Then fashioned We the drop a clot, then fashioned We the little lump bones, then clothed the bones with flesh, and then produced it as another creation, So blessed be Allah, the Best of Creators!"

[Qur'an, Surah Al-Mu'minun, 23: 12-14]

Also Surah Al-Sajdah, 32:7-9; and Surah Al-Fatir: 35: 11 can be referred in addition.

These all are the manifestation of His being **"Rabbunnas" (The Sustainer of human species].** One has to marvel at how for nine months in the darkness of the mother's womb, a child gets all means of nourishment that helps in his/her development. Then he is born as a full grown baby with all the faculties of heart and mind, strength and energies in body parts in miniature to be used when fully grown up. He/she is to continue the process of procreation towards the survival of human species and to carry out the will of his/her Creator and Sustainer on earth. It is a long drawn out process, terminating only with the commencement of **Qiyamah** (The Day of Judgment).

The **"Rahmah," the blessings** of Allah (SWT) for the human species does not end here with the miraculous process of his birth and the arrangement that He makes for his survival on earth. He did not leave him to wander in the wilderness of His uncountable living species. He created man, arranged Guidance for him, through His appointed Messengers, on how to live, act and behave on earth, and endowed him with a workable body frame, especially the placement of the **"thumb"** in his hands and the **power of expression,** to sustain him as a reasoning human being so he can survive. Allah narrates His bounties with the beginning of <u>Surah # 55, Al-Rahman, Verses 1 – 4:</u>

الرَّحْمَـنُ ـ عَلَّمَ الْقُرْآنَ ـ خَلَقَ الْإِنْسَانَ ـ عَلَّمَهُ الْبَيَانَ

"Al-Rahman, 'Allamal-Qur'an, Khalaqal-Insan, Allamahul-Bayan"

Allah created man with a beautiful body-frame wherein everything is placed in its most appropriate place and in perfect shape. He gave him a **"thumb"** for the grasping power to hold things for his service, and then **gave him the power of speech to express what he feels and thinks.** Had these two faculties not been given to man, he could not have survived on earth at all and could not have brought human civilization to its present state. Anthropologically, these are the two most essential **gifts of God** that have contributed to the progress of man. **This is the Rahmah of Allah.** The more humans express thanks to their Creator and Sustainer, the more He increases His bounties to them, as Allah ordains in the **Qur'an:**

وَإِذْ تَأَذَّنَ رَبُّكُمْ لَئِنْ شَكَرْتُمْ لَأَزِيدَنَّكُمْ ۖ وَلَئِنْ كَفَرْتُمْ إِنَّ عَذَابِي لَشَدِيدٌ

"And [Remember the time] when your Sustainer made [this promise] known: If you are grateful [to Me], I shall certainly give you more and more; but if you are ungrateful, verily, My chastisement will be severe indeed."
[Qur'an. Surah Ibrahim: 14:7]

Thus, Allah created this cosmos and what it contains for man out of His attribution of **"Al-Rahman,"** but equally and at the same time

He is **"Al-Raheem."** So, He is maintaining and sustaining it as the abode of man with all of its fascination, beauties and limitless bounties. **By virtue of that, Allah is "Rabbul 'Alameen," the Cherisher of all the worlds and species.** All the praise and thanks are, thus, reserved only for Him. If man gives credit to anyone else for these favors and bounties in any way, he/she will be committing **Shirk**, making partners with Allah's Supreme authority. That would be tantamount to a great sin and Allah never forgives **Shirk in any form.**

III. Verse # 3 – "AL-RAHMAN AL-RAHEEM":

الرَّحْمَـٰنِ الرَّحِيمِ

-The Most Gracious, the Most Kind [the Dispenser of Grace]

The previous Verse declares categorically that Allah is **"Rabbil 'Alameen."** Now this verse explains why Allah is Rabbil 'Alameen. Because He is Al-Rahman and by virtue of His being Al-Rahman, he created this cosmos, as explained earlier, while elaborating on the first Verse. But at the same time, our Lord is also Al-Raheem, and by virtue of that attribute, He is maintaining and sustaining this universe in a continuous process. That has already been explained earlier under Verse # One. Thus, being AL-Rahman and Al-Raheem, Allah is Rabbil 'Alameen.

Allah's Rahmah has no bounds or boundaries. His bounties are limitless and go beyond our imagination. He is serving our needs and urges to their minutest details round the clock right from the moment our mothers conceive us till we breathe our last. The enactment of Akhirah some day that is known to Allah alone is the extension of life beyond earth to reap the harvest of the consequences of our actions and deeds on the appointed Day of

Judgment. When that will happen only Allah knows. **The only reality is that it is an inevitable truth, the only reality on earth to encounter with utmost certainty.** Man, as His "**Abd**" should always seek His **Rahmah** in both the worlds, as without His **Rahmah**, none can enter into His **Jannah** or save his/her skin from His wrath.

IV. VERSE # 4: "MALIKEY YAWMIDDEEN":

مَالِكِ يَوْمِ الدِّين

"Lord of the Day of Judgment".

It must be clearly understood by all of us that there is no **"free-lunch"** from Allah (SWT). Allah exhorts the **Mu'mineen**:

وَأَوْفُوا بِعَهْدِي أُوفِ بِعَهْدِكُمْ وَإِيَّايَ فَارْهَبُون

"And fulfill your promise unto Me, [Whereupon] I shall fulfill My promise unto you."

[Qur'an. Surah, Al-Baqarah 2: 40]

Elsewhere Allah (SWT) ordains in **Verse # 8 of Surah # 102 – Al-**

Takathur

ثُمَّ لَتُسْأَلُنَّ يَوْمَئِذٍ عَنِ النَّعِيم

" And on that Day you will most surely be called to account for [what you did] with the bounties of life."

It means that whatever Allah has given us or entrusted us with, or showers **His blessings upon us in different shapes and manners, we all are accountable to Him for the way we use these favors on earth.** In other words, every individual human being will be asked on the Day of Judgment about what Allah entrusted to him or her - **life, time, talents, energies and resources,** and how he/she used them – the way he/she liked or the way Allah ordained for him/her to do. On that Day of Judgment none will be allowed to budge an inch from his place of accountability, unless he/she answers the following five questions as narrated by **Abi Barzah Al-Aslami and quoted by Tirmidhi**:

Rasulullah (S) said, "On the Day of Judgment none will be allowed to leave the Court of Allah (SWT) unless he (she) answers these five questions:

1. In what engagements did he (she) pass his/her (life)?
2. How far did he (she) act upon the "'Ilm" (knowledge) that he (she) acquired?
3. His wealth: from where did he earn?
4. And where did he spend it?
5. And where did he debase his body?

[Ref: Rahe 'Amal - Hadith # 386 Quoted from Tirmidhi]

It gives us an idea how serious and important that Day of Judgment will be for every individual human being where there will be no intercession in the Mightiest Court of Allah and He will be the complete Master of the situation on that Day. These basic questions cover the entire spectrum of human activities, deeds and performances on earth, the accountability of his time, talents, energies and resources. What a comprehensive accountability it will be! Only the person who would be able to say to Allah (SWT) on that Day: O Allah! What you gave me, I used all in Your way for the sake of Your pleasure, and only then he will find the paradise waiting for him.

We have to realize very consciously that the favors of Allah and His blessings are, in fact, His trust in our hands. Man is only the trustee, not the master or owner at all. For all His favors, Allah (SWT) will question us at the time when He will be the Supreme Lord of the Day. This accountability is certain

and none will be able to escape from it as Allah ordains in **Verse # 8 of Surah Al-Takathur as quoted above:**

"Thumma latusalunnah Yawma-idhin 'Anin-Na'eem"

[Then on that Day, you will be definitely asked concerning (all His) favors [and blessings]

This accountability is about the material favors of Allah. These are visible and all humans are endowed with these natural phenomenon. But what about His moral and spiritual favors that He showers upon the individual when consciously he accepts Him as his Lord, enters into His fold and concludes an open deal with Him? The responsibilities that fall upon one's shoulders after becoming a conscious Muslim or Muslimah are nothing but a Commitment between a Mu'min and the Lord of this universe, as ordained in **Verse # 111 of Surah # 9, Al-Tawbah:**

إِنَّ اللَّهَ اشْتَرَىٰ مِنَ الْمُؤْمِنِينَ أَنْفُسَهُمْ وَأَمْوَالَهُمْ بِأَنَّ لَهُمُ الْجَنَّةَ ۚ يُقَاتِلُونَ فِي سَبِيلِ اللَّهِ فَيَقْتُلُونَ وَيُقْتَلُونَ ۖ وَعْدًا عَلَيْهِ حَقًّا فِي التَّوْرَاةِ وَالْإِنْجِيلِ وَالْقُرْآنِ ۚ وَمَنْ أَوْفَىٰ بِعَهْدِهِ مِنَ اللَّهِ ۚ فَاسْتَبْشِرُوا بِبَيْعِكُمُ الَّذِي بَايَعْتُمْ بِهِ ۚ وَذَٰلِكَ هُوَ الْفَوْزُ الْعَظِيمُ

"Lo! Allah hath bought from you the believers their lives and their wealth because the Garden will be theirs; they shall fight in the way of Allah and shall slay and be slain. It is a promise which is binding on Him in the Torah and the Gospel and the Qur'an. Who fulfils his covenant better than Allah? Rejoice then in your bargain that you have made, for that is the supreme triumph."

Let us have an evaluation of these formal deals with Allah (SWT). These are the sacred trust in our hands, too, and we are accountable for each of them: Have we fulfilled our commitments to Allah or negated our obligations one way or the other?

EVALUATION OF THE COMMITMENTS OTHER THAN MATERIAL BLESSINGS:

Besides **the material and physical blessings,** Allah's favors to humanity are insurmountable, as He ordains in the **Qur'an: Verse # 18 of Al-Nahl and Verse # 34 of Surah Ibrahim:**

"And if you count the bounties of Allah, you cannot reckon it."

وَإِنْ تَعُدُّوا نِعْمَةَ اللَّهِ لَا تُحْصُوهَا ۗ إِنَّ اللَّهَ لَغَفُورٌ رَحِيمٌ

[Qur'an, Surah Al-Nahl, 16:18]

وَإِنْ تَعُدُّوا نِعْمَتَ اللَّهِ لَا تُحْصُوهَا

[Qur'an, Surah Ibrahim, 14: 34]

 Allah (SWT) appointed the human being as His "Khalifah" (Vicegerent) on earth, and harnessed all that the world contains for his exploration and use:

إِنِّي جَاعِلٌ فِي الْأَرْضِ خَلِيفَةً

"Lo! I am going to place a "Khalifah" on earth..."

[Qur'an, Surah Al-Baqarah 2: 33],

أَلَمْ تَرَوْا أَنَّ اللَّهَ سَخَّرَ لَكُمْ مَا فِي السَّمَاوَاتِ وَمَا فِي الْأَرْضِ
وَأَسْبَغَ عَلَيْكُمْ نِعَمَهُ ظَاهِرَةً وَبَاطِنَةً

"See you not how Allah has made serviceable unto you whatever is in the skies and whatever is in the earth and has loaded you with His favors both without and within?..."
[Qur'an, Surah Luqman, 31: 20]

هُوَ الَّذِي خَلَقَ لَكُمْ مَا فِي الْأَرْضِ

"He it is Who created for you all that is in earth."
[Qur'an, Surah Al-Baqarah 2: 29]

Thus, Allah made a comprehensive arrangement on earth for the survival and procreation of man. He gave man complete freedom to use His bounties the way he likes; keeping always in mind that he will be accountable to Him for all on the Day of Judgment where His authority will be total and supreme. He will judge on that Day whether humans used His bounties for the benefit of mankind in order to make their abode a cradle of peace or filled the earth with **"Zulm"** (oppression and exploitation) and **Fasad** (transgression and corruption). Accordingly, the Lord of that Day will reward or punish His **"'Abd"** (Slaves) respectively.

* **Allah (SWT)** blessed us with Guidance, gave us Tawfeeq to follow Islam and keep us on the path of righteousness. That is His greatest favor. It may pave our road towards heaven, **provided** we follow His Guidance, struggle hard for the *Iqamah (establishment) of* **His authority and Deen** throughout our life on earth, remove the **evils (Munkar)** from the society, in order to keep His earth clean from all kinds of **idolatry** and **Shirk** - associating no partner at all either with His person or to His attributes - **and establish the good (Ma'ruf) in its place, just to deliver Al-Qist (Justice) to mankind, fulfilling the ultimate mission of His Prophets and their blessed followers. The Muslim Ummah stands for the accomplishment of this mission on earth, as ordained by Allah in Verse # 25 of Surah Al-Hadeed,** and **the fulfillment of these conditions and to live by what is ordained in Surah # 3, Al-'Imran, Verse # 110 as the appointed people for these**

objectives and then live as a Jama'ah as stated in Verse # 104 of the same Surah:

كُنْتُمْ خَيْرَ أُمَّةٍ أُخْرِجَتْ لِلنَّاسِ تَأْمُرُونَ بِالْمَعْرُوفِ وَتَنْهَوْنَ عَنِ الْمُنْكَرِ وَتُؤْمِنُونَ بِاللَّهِ

"You are the best people that have been raised up for mankind. You enjoin right conduct and forbid indecency; and you believe in Allah."

[Qur'an, Surah Al-'Imran, 3: 110]

وَلْتَكُنْ مِنْكُمْ أُمَّةٌ يَدْعُونَ إِلَى الْخَيْرِ وَيَأْمُرُونَ بِالْمَعْرُوفِ وَيَنْهَوْنَ عَنِ الْمُنْكَرِ ۚ وَأُولَٰئِكَ هُمُ الْمُفْلِحُونَ

"And let there be from you a Jama'ah [a group of organized people] who invite [the mankind] to goodness [Dawah Ilal-Khayr – the Deen of Allah], and enjoin right conduct [establish Al-Ma'ruf] and forbid indecency [Al-Munkar]. Such are they who are successful."

[Qur'an, Surah Al-'Imran, 3: 104]

لَقَدْ أَرْسَلْنَا رُسُلَنَا بِالْبَيِّنَاتِ وَأَنْزَلْنَا مَعَهُمُ الْكِتَابَ وَالْمِيزَانَ لِيَقُومَ النَّاسُ بِالْقِسْطِ ۖ وَأَنْزَلْنَا الْحَدِيدَ فِيهِ بَأْسٌ شَدِيدٌ وَمَنَافِعُ لِلنَّاسِ

"We verily sent our Messengers with clear proofs, and revealed with them the Scripture and the Balance that mankind may observe right measures (Al-Qist) and He revealed iron, wherein is mighty power and (many) uses for mankind."
[Qur'an, Surah Al-Hadeed, 57:25]

It was the paramount mission of all the Messengers of Allah to fulfill on earth. The Torah, the Zabur, the Bible and the **Qur'an** have the same message **as without Justice no peace and security could**

<u>be guaranteed on earth.</u> All human beings, especially Muslims *[Jews and Christians too **were originally Muslims, being the followers of Abrahamic faith**]*, <u>are answerable to their Creator and Sustainer</u> as to what part they played or are playing in fulfilling this topmost mission of their existence on earth. It is the lifelong pursuit of a Muslim to meet these conditions on earth. It is incumbent upon him to leave no stone unturned to get it established. However, the mission would never be possible to attain without establishing the Divine Guidance that was brought each time by the Messenger of Allah. Only in its wake could human society be engulfed with justice, peace and security all around.

- So the establishment of Allah's Deen and the prevalence of Justice and peace go together as the latter cannot emerge without the enactment of the former requisite. In other words, to have Justice and peace on earth, His Divine Guidance must be established on this earth as a prelude to Justice. <u>**Howsoever human society and the international institutions may cry or agitate for peace and security on earth, it will never see the light of the day if the Deen of Allah is not established on earth as a political entity.**</u> All the Messengers/Prophets of the time struggled for it and their benevolent followers carried it out as their mission to the extent possible on their part as the sole objective of their individual and collective life. On the Day of Judgment both the Messengers and their respective **Ummah** will be asked to explain their respective position. <u>To the Messengers:</u>

"Have you delivered the Message in its totality and demonstrated your life-pattern as its model? And <u>to the respective Ummah</u>: "How did you respond?"

The concluding Verses of <u>**Surah # 5, Al-Maidah, Verses # 116 to 119,**</u> give a vivid picture of that accountability in Akhirah.

وَإِذْ قَالَ اللَّهُ يَا عِيسَى ابْنَ مَرْيَمَ أَأَنْتَ قُلْتَ لِلنَّاسِ اتَّخِذُونِي وَأُمِّيَ إِلَٰهَيْنِ مِنْ دُونِ اللَّهِ ۖ قَالَ سُبْحَانَكَ مَا يَكُونُ لِي أَنْ أَقُولَ مَا لَيْسَ

لِي بِحَقٍّ ۚ إِنْ كُنْتُ قُلْتُهُ فَقَدْ عَلِمْتَهُ ۚ تَعْلَمُ مَا فِي نَفْسِي وَلَا أَعْلَمُ مَا فِي نَفْسِكَ ۚ إِنَّكَ أَنْتَ عَلَّامُ الْغُيُوبِ

مَا قُلْتُ لَهُمْ إِلَّا مَا أَمَرْتَنِي بِهِ أَنِ اعْبُدُوا اللَّهَ رَبِّي وَرَبَّكُمْ ۚ وَكُنْتُ عَلَيْهِمْ شَهِيدًا مَا دُمْتُ فِيهِمْ ۖ فَلَمَّا تَوَفَّيْتَنِي كُنْتَ أَنْتَ الرَّقِيبَ عَلَيْهِمْ ۚ وَأَنْتَ عَلَىٰ كُلِّ شَيْءٍ شَهِيدٌ

إِنْ تُعَذِّبْهُمْ فَإِنَّهُمْ عِبَادُكَ ۖ وَإِنْ تَغْفِرْ لَهُمْ فَإِنَّكَ أَنْتَ الْعَزِيزُ الْحَكِيمُ قَالَ اللَّهُ هَٰذَا يَوْمُ يَنْفَعُ الصَّادِقِينَ صِدْقُهُمْ ۚ لَهُمْ جَنَّاتٌ تَجْرِي مِنْ تَحْتِهَا الْأَنْهَارُ خَالِدِينَ فِيهَا أَبَدًا ۚ رَضِيَ اللَّهُ عَنْهُمْ وَرَضُوا عَنْهُ ۚ ذَٰلِكَ الْفَوْزُ الْعَظِيمُ

"And when Allah said: O Jesus, son of Mary! Didst thou say unto mankind; Take me and my mother for the two gods beside Allah? He said: Be glorified! It was not mine to utter that to which I had no right. If I used to say it, then You knew it. You knew what is in my mind, and I know not what is in Thy mind. Lo! You, only You are the Knower of Things Hidden."

"I spoke unto them only that which You commanded me, (saying): Worship Allah, my Lord and your Lord. I was a witness of them while I dwelt among them, and when You took me You were the Watcher over them. You are Witness over all things."

"If You punish them: lo! They are Thy slaves, and if You forgive them (lo! they are Thy slaves). Lo! You, only You are the Mighty, the Wise."

"Allah said: This is a day in which their truthfulness profits the truthful, for theirs are the Gardens underneath which rivers

*flow, wherein they are secure forever. Allah taking pleasure in
them and they in Him. That is the great triumph."*

[Surah Al-Maidah, 5: 116 -119]

No believer, no Muslim would be immune from this process. That
would be the Day of **Jaza'** (reward or punishment); the day of
accountability, and our Lord will be the Supreme Master with total
authority. No intercession and no ransom will be possible on that
day. **Our Lord will be: MALIKEY YAWMIDDIN, the Supreme
Lord of the Day. Warnings in the Qur'an are very clear in this
respect:**

فَلَنَسْأَلَنَّ الَّذِينَ أُرْسِلَ إِلَيْهِمْ وَلَنَسْأَلَنَّ الْمُرْسَلِينَ
فَلَنَقُصَّنَّ عَلَيْهِمْ بِعِلْمٍ ۖ وَمَا كُنَّا غَائِبِينَ

*"Then verily We will question those unto whom (our
Messengers) had been sent and verily We shall question the
Messengers. Then verily We shall narrate unto them (the
event) with knowledge, for verily We were not absent (when it
came to pass)."*
[Qur'an, Surah Al-A'raf, 7: 6-7]

**[Also in Surah Baqarah, Verses 48 and 123 can be referred to
in this respect.]**

Those who will come out successful, victorious, on that Day of
Judgment will be **"selected or awarded"** by Allah the
"Citizenship" of Paradise in the next world after Resurrection, the
place of eternal bliss; and those who will cut sorry figures on that
Day will be thrown in the ditch of eternal fire, the place of
continuous and perpetual torment and torture. **What an eventful
day it will be! Allah (SWT) is making us feel conscious of the
horrors of that Day so that we correct our ways and work hard
on earth to earn His pleasure. Elsewhere, the Qur'an describes
human's total "hopelessness" on that Day in these words:**

وَمَا أَدْرَاكَ مَا يَوْمُ الدِّينِ

ثُمَّ مَا أَدْرَاكَ مَا يَوْمُ الدِّينِ

يَوْمَ لَا تَمْلِكُ نَفْسٌ لِنَفْسٍ شَيْئًا ۖ وَالْأَمْرُ يَوْمَئِذٍ لِلَّهِ

"And what could make you conceive what that Judgment Day will be?
And once again: what could make you conceive what that Judgment Day will be?
[It would be] a day when no human being shall be of the least avail to another human being: for on that day [it will become manifest that] all sovereignty is Allah's alone."

[Qur'an, Surah Al-Infitar, 82: 17 – 19]

DISASTROUS SITUATION ON THE DAY OF JUDGMENT:

Repentance of any kind on that Day will bear no fruit at all. No excuse will come to the help of the disbelievers, the ungrateful, the thankless, the idolaters, the **Mushrikeen** (those who make partners with Allah in His person or in His attributes) and the transgressors. All these people will be in unprecedented trouble, finding no escape from it. If one could envision the horrible panorama of the situation at the time of accountability, he/she will tremble and shiver right away. **The state of 'hearing" and its intensity in the Court of Allah on that Day can be visualized through this Hadith of Rasulullah (S), narrated both by Bukhari and Muslim:**

"Rasulullah (S) said, "Each one of you will have direct assembly (underline)individually(/underline) with Allah (SWT- at the time of Accountability) and he/she will have no translator, no recommendatory and no helper except his deeds, and nothing will be at his/her hands.

When this person will look towards his right, he will find nothing coming to his rescue except his deeds;

And when he will look to his left, he will find nothing coming to his help except his deeds;

He will then look to his front, and he will find bursting hellfire with all its devastating horrible state.

O People! Have concern to protect your selves from hellfire even by giving half a date (in His way to the have-nots)."

- **Treatment of the hypocrites:** It will be the worst for them on that Day. See the scenario as depicted in this Hadith, narrated by Abu Hurairah (RA) and produced by Muslim:

Rasulullah (S) said, "On the Day of Qiyamah (the Day of Judgment) a person will come to his Lord, and He will ask him: have I not given you honor and respect; have I not given you wife, horses, camels and respite, were you not running your administration and collecting tolls?
He will say, "Definitely" [Confirming all the blessings that he was favored with.]
He will then be asked, "Did you not expect to face Me"?
He will say, "No."
In response, Allah will say, "The way you forgot Me (in the world) likewise I will forget you today."
Another person will come forward and face the same dialogue (with Allah).
Then a third person will come and he will face the same questions as the previous two faced (who were disbelievers).
This (third) person will respond: I believed in You, I used to offer Salah, was fasting and used to spend my wealth in Your way. [Rasulullah (S) added that he will recount likewise many of his (so-called) "good deeds" with great emphasis].
Allah (SWT) will tell him, "Stop," and will say, "I will just call witness against you." He will then say to himself: Who will be witness against me (here)?
His lips will then be sealed (because he will not be ashamed of speaking lies even in the presence of Allah, as he was beating

false drums of his piousness in the world before the Messenger and Muslims).

His thigh, his flesh and his bones will be questioned (about his worldly deeds). All will describe/expose truthfully the mockery of his (so-called) deeds. Thus, Allah will shut the door of his excuses and mockeries.

Rasulullah (S) added, "He is the person who was a hypocrite (Munafiq) in the world and on whom the wrath of Allah will fall." [From Rah-e-'Amal: Hadith # 32 – The end-result of hypocrites]

- **Concern For Akhirah:** Keeping the above scenario in mind, our concern for Akhirah should always be at its highest peak, when we will be asked about what we are enjoying on earth; about all the favors that Allah is showering upon us for our survival; about the **Amanah** (trust) that we hold, regarding our commitments that we undertake, and the enormous obligations that we carry on our shoulders as fathers, mothers, sons, daughters, neighbors and citizens of a society. On every count we are accountable to Allah as to how we fulfill our responsibilities. It will be a very trying and difficult Day for every individual human being. The greater the quantum of **Amanah** in one's hands, the larger will be the scope of accountability.

:

* **The voting power that we have is a trust in our hands**– how we used it and whom we entrusted, for the good of humanity or for creating more corruption in human society through empowering corrupt leadership;

* **The political power that we hold** – how we used it in making human society a boon for the poor, the oppressed and the have-nots, **or** a source of exploitation of others: an abode of peace and security, or a place of corruption and disorder for the people;

* **Allah (SWT) will definitely ask: In the context of today's world, the lands on which I gave you authority or the sovereign rights to rule, control and govern the affairs of 57**

predominantly Muslim countries on earth, what system have you introduced there? Have you established My authority and the Islamic System of life that I accepted for you as your Deen? How have you used the resources that I gave you: for the betterment of your people or squandered away on your luxuries? It will be a very hard time for the Muslim leadership to answer these very fundamental questions that will be put to them on that fateful Day and the governing coterie of each Muslim country.   Allah's directives are very clear in this respect:

الَّذِينَ إِنْ مَكَّنَّاهُمْ فِي الْأَرْضِ أَقَامُوا الصَّلَاةَ وَآتَوُا الزَّكَاةَ وَأَمَرُوا بِالْمَعْرُوفِ وَنَهَوْا عَنِ الْمُنْكَرِ ۗ وَلِلَّهِ عَاقِبَةُ الْأُمُورِ

"Those who, if We give them power in the land [firmly establish them on earth], establish Salah, pay Zakah (the poor-due] and enjoin Ma'ruf [of doing what is right] and forbid the Munkar [the doing of what is wrong]. And with Allah rests the final outcome of all events."

[Qur'an, Surah Al-Hajj, 22: 41]

* **The wealth that Allah gave you** - how and where you used it: hording and multiplying for wrongful means of exploitation through fraud, speculation, squeezing the people and society on lending it on interest or spending it for the poor, the needy, the deprived and in the way of Allah to earn His pleasure;
* **The time, the talents, the energies and the resources that Allah gave you** – where you used each of them: in the service of **Batil** (evil forces): promoting and building the corrupt system of your respective societies, in strengthening the corrupt socio-economic-political order of the day **or** in the promotion and establishing the Truth, the Deen of Allah on earth, in earning your livelihood through honest and rightful means of living? It will be a very crucial and critical question for every human being to answer;

* **The Guidance that Allah sent to you in a continuous process** through His appointed Messengers in a chain for making the human society an abode of peace, order, justice and fair play. What was your treatment of this Guidance: an attitude of total negation or partial acceptance or of total acceptance? How did you behave with My Prophet of the time? Have you refused him out of your arrogance or followed him with love and respect?

* Did you accept Allah's authority on earth and carve out your affairs in terms of the Guidance that He sent to you, or did you make your God a personal God, or your God as a human god, or did you coin a lot of gods and goddesses as god-incarnate out of My creations and fill the earth with **Fasad** (disorder), idolatry, **Shirk [making partners with Allah either in His authority or His attributes]** and transgression and, thus, lose the guidance in its wake?

These fatal scenarios would be very hard to envision by an individual unless he fills his heart and mind with a profound sense of gratitude for the favors and bounties that Allah has showered upon him for the sustenance of our species on this earth, and he feels always accountable to Him for each and every thing that he holds, possesses and uses of this cosmos.

Our Lord is Supreme and I am answerable to Him. This sense of accountability must run in our body, mind and soul with every breath that we inhale in the manner blood is running in our veins and arteries. It would make each human being on earth an extremely responsible identity, shivering always under the conscious pressure of accountability. Only such men and women will be able to face and say to the Lord of the Day of Judgment - "Ma'likey Yawmiddeen": O my Lord! What ever you gave me, I spend it all in Your way and for your pleasure only. Falah or success will be waiting only for these fortunate few. The rest will be the losers and the doomed.

CHAPTER - 2

V. VERSE # 5: IYYAKA NA'BUDU WA IYYAKA NASTA'EEN:

إِيَّاكَ نَعْبُدُ وَإِيَّاكَ نَسْتَعِينُ

Translation: You alone do we worship; and unto You alone we turn for help.

This is one of the capsule **verses** of the **Qur'an,** where in a few precise words Allah (SWT) has engulfed an ocean of meanings in depth. This verse embodies total surrender to Allah (SWT); the manifestation of complete dependence on Him alone; a verse holding and conveying the most puritan concept of Monotheism **(Tawheediyah**), guiding to the surest way to attain the total favor of Allah if it is practiced in its true letter and spirit by the Muslims. **It is an eternal source of paramount guidance in every aspect of our socio-economic and political life both at individual and collective levels.**

If Muslims around the world could have made this meaningful verse as the barometer of their life-pattern, they would have been able to change the prevailing gloom, despondency and frustration of their existence on earth into everlasting glory long ago. They would never have been targeted and pronounced as "terrorist" by any Bush, Blaire or Zionist. They would never have been found roaming on the streets of Europe and America with beggar's bowl in hand asking for "help," "protection," financial aid and technical know-how. They would have never been subjugated either by the world colonial powers sustaining imperial designs or their own despotic, opportunistic military rulers. In consequence, the history of the Muslim world would have been quite different today. Conversely, the world would have been "ever-coming" to them "begging" for help, guidance, "Salvation" and seeking solutions to its lifelong problems.

Let us see what this **verse** contains in its depth in the background of the preceding verses of **Al-Fatiha** and what it connotes with extraordinary emphasis on all the believers to practice as the golden living principle of our earthly life.

* **The Background of this verse:** At the very outset the **'Abd of Allah** (His slave] very humbly accepts with all eloquence His favors and bounties in the creation of man and this cosmos for him and for his maintenance on earth on account of His being **Al-Rahman and Al- Raheem**. These feelings of **assertion** fill his heart with an extreme sense of gratitude and make him express that all thanks and gratefulness are for Allah, the Sustainer of all the worlds: **"Al-Hamdu Lillahey Rabbil A'lameen."** This confirmation is the echo of his heart that surrenders to Him in all servitude, profoundly acknowledging the care and constant looking after His species, and realizing fully well that His favors and magnanimity are **NOT FREE**. One day this universe will come to an end and that will be the Day of Judgment, All human beings will attend His Court of Justice **compulsorily** and be accountable to Him about what they did while living on His earth. That would be the Day of Resurrection and the authority of our Lord will be Supreme. After this assertion, His 'Abd' (servant) surrenders to Him declaring categorically: **"You alone do we worship; and unto You alone we turn for help".** *It is a big declaration and a lifelong binding statement on the part of a Muslim and a Muslimah to live by that.*

* Iyyaka Na'budu:

إِيَّاكَ نَعْبُدُ

By putting the **"predicate"** or the **"objective"** in the forefront, this expression created the concept of **total surrender** to Allah (SWT).with total reliance on Him, making worship (**Ibadah**), or total obedience, for Allah alone. Here **"Ibadah"** stands for the total obedience to Allah in every walk of life. By virtue of this declaration man, the servant of God commits himself to obey Him and His directives alone in all forms and conditions. It positively negates all forms of **Shirk** and makes **'Ibadah** (worship) pure for Allah alone.

"Na'budu" is derived from **"'Ibadah"** which means to express obedience or prostrating before someone in all sublime humility with extreme love and reverence. Thus, the concept of **'Ibadah** in Islam is all pervasive, comprehensive and total, covering the entire spectrum of human life. So, **"'Ibadah"** does not stand only for some formats of prayers or **Sawm** (fasting), or some religious rituals as it is commonly understood by the so-called traditional Muslims.

Imam Ghazali (RA), in his thought-provoking book **"Arba'een,"** **has described that "'Ibadah" consists of ten items, or categories, wherein obedience to Allah is to be strictly observed.** They are as follows:

1. **Salah;**
2, **Zakah;**
3. **Sawm;**
4. **Hajj;**
5. **Study of the Qur'an;**
6. **Remembrance of Allah under all conditions;**
7. **Making every effort for Rizq-al-Halal (honest means of living);**
8. **Being mindful of the rights of neighbors and partners or companions;**
9. **Enjoining the doing of what is right (Ma'ruf);**
10. **Forbidding the doing of what is wrong (Munkar)**
[Ref: Maa'riful Qur'an - Mufti Mohammad Shafi Saheb –page 86-87 Vol. 1: Tafseer Surah Al-Fatiha]

This is a panoramic vision of Muslim Life. It covers every aspect of human life both in individual and collective spheres, and that in every sphere a Muslim obeys his Creator and Sustainer and follows His directives towards the betterment of human life on earth, fostering justice and fair play in every walk of life. If he does not fulfill these conditions, the state of his **"'Ubudiyah" (servitude to**

Allah] will remain or stand incomplete, partial or neglected, whereas Allah (SWT) ordains the believers:

يَا أَيُّهَا الَّذِينَ آمَنُوا ادْخُلُوا فِي السِّلْمِ كَافَّةً وَلَا تَتَّبِعُوا خُطُوَاتِ الشَّيْطَانِ ۚ إِنَّهُ لَكُمْ عَدُوٌّ مُبِينٌ

"Ya Ayyuhalladhina Amanu Udkhulu Fis-Silmi Kaffatan wa la Tattabi'u khutuwatish-Shaytan: Innahu lakum aduwwun mubeen"

[O ye who believe! Come all of you into submission (unto Him - in Islam); and follow not Shaytan's footsteps, for, verily, he is your open enemy.]

[Qur'an, Surah Al-Baqarah, 2: 208]

QUR'AN CONFIRMS THIS COMPREHENSIVE CONCEPT OF UBUDIYAH:

In fact, **Iman** is a commitment, a deal between Allah and His **'Abd** (slave). By committing to **La Ilaha Ilallah** a Muslim surrenders his/her life and wealth to Allah in hopes of **Jannah**:

إِنَّ اللَّهَ اشْتَرَىٰ مِنَ الْمُؤْمِنِينَ أَنْفُسَهُمْ وَأَمْوَالَهُمْ بِأَنَّ لَهُمُ الْجَنَّةَ ۚ يُقَاتِلُونَ فِي سَبِيلِ اللَّهِ فَيَقْتُلُونَ وَيُقْتَلُونَ ۖ وَعْدًا عَلَيْهِ حَقًّا فِي التَّوْرَاةِ وَالْإِنْجِيلِ وَالْقُرْآنِ ۚ وَمَنْ أَوْفَىٰ بِعَهْدِهِ مِنَ اللَّهِ ۚ فَاسْتَبْشِرُوا بِبَيْعِكُمُ الَّذِي بَايَعْتُمْ بِهِ ۚ وَذَٰلِكَ هُوَ الْفَوْزُ الْعَظِيمُ

"Lo! Allah has bought from the believers their lives and their wealth in lieu of paradise (Jannah] that will be theirs; they shall fight in the way of Allah and shall slay and be slain. It is a promise that is binding on Him in the Torah and the Gospel and the Qur'an. Who fulfills his covenant better than Allah? Rejoice then in your bargain that ye have made, for that is the supreme triumph."
[Qur'an, Surah Al- Tawbah, 9-111]

The overall nature of this **Iman**, this commitment, has been amply described by Allah in the next **Verse # 112 of Surah Al-Tawbah.** It covers the entire spectrum of human life and all aspects of the life of a **Mu'min** (believer) on earth as to how he acts, lives and behaves towards attaining the pleasure of Allah, and that would be the supreme triumph for him/ (her):

التَّائِبُونَ الْعَابِدُونَ الْحَامِدُونَ السَّائِحُونَ الرَّاكِعُونَ السَّاجِدُونَ
الْآمِرُونَ بِالْمَعْرُوفِ
وَالنَّاهُونَ عَنِ الْمُنْكَرِ وَالْحَافِظُونَ لِحُدُودِ اللَّهِ ۗ وَبَشِّرِ الْمُؤْمِنِينَ

"(Triumphant) are those who turn repentant (to Allah), those who worship (Him), those who praise (Him), those who fast [or go on and on seeking His goodly acceptance], those who bow down before (Him) and prostrate themselves in adoration, those who enjoin the right (Ma'ruf) and who forbid the doing of what is wrong (Munkar) and those who keep to the bonds set by Allah. And give You [O Prophet] the glad tidings [of God's promise] to the believers."

[Qur'an, Surah Al-Tawbah, 9: 112]

A Muslim must always be mindful of his/her commitment to Allah that he/she has to follow only Him in every walk of life, irrespective of where he/she is and what he/she is doing and with what circumstances he/she is surrounded by. Only then will he/she be able to fulfill the condition of total **"Ubudiyah"** (submission) on earth. This submission will not be for one day but for the entire life till he/she breathes his/her last.

However, Muslims are very much unmindful of this paramount condition of their Iman; they do violate it every now and then, not only in personal life but in every aspect of their social, economic and political life. As such, they all [with a few exceptions here and there] are grossly violating their commitment to Allah and **then** expect that Allah will come to their help when they call upon Him.

The entire Muslim Ummah has been infested with this flagrant violation for centuries in a continuous process, while begging for His mercy and Nusrah at the same time. What a great anomalous situation it is! Both the Muslim Ummah and its highly educated intelligentsia, the so-called "Muslim scholars," do not realize their self-created and extraordinarily self-contradictory position and do something positive to get the situation corrected. In consequence, the sufferings of the Ummah are multiplying manifold day in and day out.

There are **57** predominantly Muslim countries, but nowhere is Allah's Deen dominant in the body politics of any of these countries. Their system of education, economic layouts, political set ups, and international relations; all are based on laws and systems that are repugnant to Allah's **Deen** and His **Shariah** [the Code of conduct prescribed by Islam to run the affairs of the **Ummah** at each level of society]. Why, then, should Allah give them honor and dignity in the community of nations? Muslims just follow Him only in some "outward" ritualistic manifestation of some worship (**'Ibadah**), virtually "locking" Him up or restricting His **'Ibadah** in the four walls of their **Masjid**, taking His name customarily on some occasions and following the secular un-Islamic laws in all aspects of their life. This condition naturally constantly invites His wrath. The perpetuation of this state of affairs continues in spite of His categorical warning:

أَفَتُؤْمِنُونَ بِبَعْضِ الْكِتَابِ وَتَكْفُرُونَ بِبَعْضٍ ۚ فَمَا جَزَاءُ مَنْ يَفْعَلُ ذَٰلِكَ مِنْكُمْ إِلَّا خِزْيٌ فِي الْحَيَاةِ الدُّنْيَا ۖ وَيَوْمَ الْقِيَامَةِ يُرَدُّونَ إِلَىٰ أَشَدِّ الْعَذَابِ ۗ وَمَا اللَّهُ بِغَافِلٍ عَمَّا تَعْمَلُونَ

"Believe you in part of the Scripture and disbelieve in part thereof? And what is the reward of those who do so save ignominy in the life of the world and on the Day of Resurrection they will be consigned to the most grievous doom. For <u>Allah is not unaware of what you do.</u>"
[Qur'an, Surah Al-Baqarah, 2: 85}

So, Allah is watching all our actions and deeds as to how we, the Muslims, as a people are neglecting, ignoring or sidetracking His directives [His **Hidayah** (guidance)) and, in consequence, we are reaping the harvest of ignominy that we are sowing by our own hands. Muslims cannot change their fate, their condition, unless they fulfill their commitment to Allah that **only Allah we all worship and follow only the Deen, the system of life that He has ordained for us.**

This Verse # 5, under discussion, has two component parts: One is total surrender to Allah and complete obedience to Him and following the Guidance that He had sent for us in its minutest details in the way it was followed and demonstrated by Rasulullah (S) and his (S) beloved companions in their respective life pattern which is now the only perfect model for the **Ummah** to follow under all eventualities and for all times to come.

In a **Hadith-al-Qudsi [which I will discuss and share, Insha Allah, in detail at a later stage]** narrated by Abu Hurairah (RA) and quoted by Muslim, Allah (SWT) has divided this **Verse** between Him and His 'Abd and says: "**My 'Abd will get what he/she will beg form Me**." This is an undertaking or a promise from the Lord of this Universe and it would never go unfulfilled, but, unfortunately, it is the Muslim **Ummah** that is not proving worthy of this immaculate conditional commitment of its Sustainer.

The second part of Verse # 5 is equally of paramount importance.

- WA IYYAKA NASTA'EEN - *Unto You alone we turn for help:*

وَإِيَّاكَ نَسْتَعِينُ

"**Nasta'een**" is derived from "**Isti'anah**" – to seek help from someone.
The emphasis here, again, is on the "**Predicate,**" keeping the objective in the forefront and, therefore, *it carries the sense of*

entrusting all our needs and urgencies to Allah (SWT) or begging from Him alone for acceptance.

One may seek help in any form and for anything, but he must beg it from Allah (SWT) and none other. Thereby, a Muslim commits himself/herself to entrust all his/her needs and urgencies only to Allah.

When a Muslim begs:

"Rizq" (sustenance) for survival;
"'Ilm" (knowledge) both of Deen and of this cosmos;
"Hidayah" (Guidance) on how to act, live and behave on this earth;
"Health" to continue his struggle for His Deen to the last breathe;
"Appealing manners" to live with harmony with others:
"Honest means of living" and Barakah in it to maintain his family in the way
   acceptable to Him;
"A tongue" that always glorifies Him;
"A heart" that is always filled deep with adoration for Him and with humility; and,
"Ever-lasting Love" for our beloved Prophet Rasulullah (S);
"Courage, Sabr and Wisdom" to stand by Haqq against oppression, trials and tribulations that are inevitable while struggling in the path of righteousness; and
"Tawfeeq" (Allah's favor) to carry out the mission of life towards the Iqamah (establishment) of Allah's Deen on earth as a political entity in the political realm and beyond;

he/she must seek and beg all and everything only and only from Allah (SWT), the Lord of this cosmos.

No king, no queen, no parliament, no president, no senate, no congress, no bank, no corporation, no mighty general and no so-called "sovereign" people can give anything to anyone howsoever powerful it or he may claim to be, individually or collectively. All beg

from Him, the Supreme Lord of this universe. Man has no option but to keep beseeching and imploring before the Lord God, irrespective of time, age, place and position. **The Muslim, by virtue of his Iman in Allah (SWT), stands committed to beg only from Him. That is what <u>"Iyyaka Nasta'een"</u> connotes and a Muslim has to abide by it and live by it with all its intents and purposes.**
However, the behavior of the Muslim **Ummah** in this respect is quite deplorable and tragic. Every Muslim and Muslimah commits and confesses at least 17 times in obligatory **Salah** every day: **"You alone we do worship and from You alone we seek help,"** but in action many mostly negate it every day and most of the time. Our socio-economic-political life presents a different picture. We turn our face from Allah (SWT) to some Peers, some saints, some graves, and some Sufi's chains and put their grievances, urges and desires to them for fulfillment. and commit **Shirk** knowingly that none of these "agencies" can fulfill his/her prayers.

Last year during Hajj time, a brother from Lahore, Pakistan, while doing **"Tawaf"** around the House of Allah, was urging his family in Lahore on his cell phone to go to "DATA DARBAR" [the grave of a Sufi saint in Lahore] and pray for the acceptance of his 'Hajj" which he was performing in the House of Allah. Could there be anything more offensive to Allah than this ignorant act of His slave while he is in His House begging others to intercede in his prayers for their acceptance? This story was published in Pakistani papers and the Muslim world was stunned to read it. **This anomalous situation prevails in the personal life pattern of Muslims in many Muslim countries of Asia and Africa.** They do not fulfill the undertaking that they perform individually to Allah in their respective prayers. It makes their **'Ibadah** and devotion to Allah a lifeless objective and their assertion to seek help only from Allah becomes meaningless and a mere mockery in effect. Allah (SWT) does not need such "exercises" in futility.

This position, in fact, becomes more pathetic and contradictory when we examine the condition of the Muslim **Ummah** in its collective sphere. We have the most accomplished system of life –

Al-Deen Al-Islam to shape our personal, family and socio-economic-political system to develop our society in peace, harmony and balance. But Muslims as nation states are looking towards socialism, capitalism and liberal democracy for the solution to their social evils, economic injustices and political upheavals. It is the most flagrant violation of our declaration as believers. Allah (SWT) categorically affirms that:

"Inna al-Deena 'ind-Allahi Al-Islam," [إِنَّ الدِّينَ عِنْدَ اللَّهِ الْإِسْلَامُ (Qur'an, Surah Al 'Imran, 3:19)) — The true System of life (AL-Deen) in the sight of Allah is Al-Islam (self surrender unto Him),** but nowhere in the Muslim world is it in a dominant position, though Allah (SWT) clearly **warns:**

وَمَنْ يَبْتَغِ غَيْرَ الْإِسْلَامِ دِينًا فَلَنْ يُقْبَلَ مِنْهُ وَهُوَ فِي الْآخِرَةِ مِنَ الْخَاسِرِينَ

"Those whoso seek the system of life other than Deen Al-Islam, it would never be accepted from them and they will be the losers in both the worlds."
[Qur'an, Surah Al-'Imran. 3: 85]

In short, what we categorically assert in our Salah while reciting Al-Fatiha and in supplication, we contradict our assertion through our actions, behavior and performances. Neither do Muslims surrender and show their "'Ubudiyah" alone to Allah in every aspect of life, nor do they seek Nusrah [His help and protection] in every walk of life for their needs and difficulties. Thus, their life stands as a jumble of contradictions and inconsistencies, and Allah (SWT) has no interest in responding to their prayers. The beautiful way ordained by Allah for His " 'ABD" to come closer to Him through Al-Fatiha in a continuous process day in and day out, living constantly under the shadow of His mercy and Nusrah [His help and protection] is being hopelessly lost by Muslims. The Salah that could bring us closer to Allah, elevate us in His sight and that of the community of nations is not helping us at all due to our own negligence and carelessness.

CHAPTER - 3

VI. Verse # 6. "EHDINA AL-SIRAT-AL-MUSTAQEEMA"

اهْدِنَا الصِّرَاطَ الْمُسْتَقِيمَ

[O Allah! Guide us or show us [and keep us on] the straight path.]

The word **"Hidayah"** has been elaborated on by Imam Raghib Asphani in his book **Mafradat-ul Qur'an** as: "to guide someone to his destiny with kindness and care." However, it must be noted carefully that guidance comes from Allah alone and it comes in different forms and shapes that vary from species to species.

"Ehdina" does not mean alone **"show us the right path,"** but it connotes: console our heart with its correctness; grace us with enthusiasm to walk along with it; ease for us the hurdles **[trials and tribulations]** that are inevitable in this path; and protect us from deviation to other paths after keeping us on the straight path. All these connotations have crept in it after withdrawing **"Silah" (Conjunction)**. It made the concept of **"Ehdina"** all comprehensive **[Ref: Tadabbur-al-Qur'an – Amin Ahsan Islahi Vol. 1 page 15]**

"AL- Sirat Al- Mustaqeem" – The **Straight Path** that Allah (SWT) has fixed or designated for humans through His appointed Messengers to follow in this world for **leading a balanced and harmonious life** on earth and to attain success **(Falah)** in both the worlds, protecting man always from falling into the ditches of Shaytanic deviations of **"Khusran"** (failure or loss). Man is likely to encounter these paths of deviation at any time, as Shaytan and his disciples are always targeting man to entrap him within their pitfalls.

Rasulullah (S) one day made a point on the ground before his (S) beloved companions (RA) and called it **"Dunya"** (the world) and put another point calling it **"Jannah" (paradise),** connected these two points with a straight line and said: There is one and only one straight path (**"Sirat-al-Mustaqeem"**) that leads one to Paradise. This **"Sirat-al-Mustaqeem"** is surrounded with a lot of zigzag and erratic lanes, by-lanes or shortcuts, the Shaytanic paths of deviation that lead man only to Hellfire. The Qur'an has termed that straight path as **"Sawaa-al-Sabeel."** [**Qur'an, Surah Al-Maidah. 5:12**]

فَمَنْ كَفَرَ بَعْدَ ذَلِكَ مِنْكُمْ فَقَدْ ضَلَّ سَوَاءَ السَّبِيلِ

The Crooked or Deviated Paths: Those who deny the **Hidayah,** the Straight Path from their Creator and Sustainer, never get peace in this life, live in suffocation, wander aimlessly in this world and follow this or that man-made law or system. In this process they never get on the straight path to balance their life, give solace to their heart and mind, attain contentment in life, or get on the path leading to eternal bliss in heaven. They lose success, **"Falah,"** in both the worlds and only meet **"Khusran"** (failure) as their ultimate destiny.

For some time they live on certain man-made systems, serving many realities or urges of life   [we can call it the **"thesis"** of life) while denying at the same time many others [we can **call them: "anti-thesis"**]. In consequence, they make a reverse gear in life and follow the neglected realities or urges while, in the process, they deprive their lives with some other truths or needs as they do not have the Divine Guidance to lead a perfect life in harmony. Thus, those who turn their face away from the Guidance from their Creator and Sustainer run blindly from one pole to another and never reach the light, the straight path of righteousness, and end their lives in confusion and darkness of ignorance through which they were running from one extreme to another for the whole of their lives. Our Sustainer, in His infinite mercy, has not left us to grapple in darkness and ignorance. **He has arranged the truthful Guidance, the straight path ["Sirat-al-Mustaqeem"], in a continuous process through the chain of His appointed**

Messengers and we beg from Him to show us and keep us on that path all throughout our existence on earth.

The question arises: **Is Guidance not the most urgent and the greatest need of man on earth?** Man needs it at every moment/step of his life. He cannot live without Divine Guidance at all. This question needs elaboration in depth as the most significant question of our life on earth.

- Complexities of Hidayah: Kinds of Hidayah (Guidance) are many and vary from species to species.

* General Guidance: We can call it as Natural Instincts. That is given to all the animate and inanimate objects of this cosmos that include animals, plants, trees, birds and insects etc. It is in their genes and all act, live, behave and survive as per their respective natural instincts. As such, this universe is running very smoothly without any confusion, disturbance, disarray and overlapping of one over the other in a strict, orderly fashion. All are meticulously following their given instincts and fulfilling the objective for which they are created by the Supreme Lord of this universe. Allah ordains this fact categorically in **Verse # 2 of Surah # 25, Al-Furqan:**

وَخَلَقَ كُلَّ شَيْءٍ فَقَدَّرَهُ تَقْدِيرًا

"And He Who creates every thing and determines its nature [destiny] in accordance with [His own] design." [In accordance with functions assigned by Him to each individual thing or phenomenon] – Explanatory note given by Mohammad Asad in his Commentary: The Message of the Qur'an p 549]

سَبِّح اسْمَ رَبِّكَ الْأَعْلَى - الَّذِي خَلَقَ فَسَوَّىٰ

"Who creates [every thing], and thereupon forms it in accordance with what it is meant to be; and who determines the nature [of all that exists], and thereupon guides it [towards its fulfillment.]

[Qur'an, Surah Al-A'la, *7: 2-3]

٨٧ ١-٢

In response to the question of Pharaoh: *"Who is your Sustainer, O Moses?"*

قَالَ فَمَنْ رَبُّكُمَا يَا مُوسَىٰ

قَالَ رَبُّنَا الَّذِي أَعْطَىٰ كُلَّ شَيْءٍ خَلْقَهُ ثُمَّ هَدَىٰ

"He replied, Our Sustainer is He who gives unto every thing [that exists] its true nature and form, and thereupon guides it (towards its fulfillment)."

[Qur'an, Surah Ta Ha, 20: 49 -50]

The above quotes from the **Qur'an** prove that this cosmos is controlled and guided meticulously by the Creator and Sustainer and hence, there is no question of any **"Clash of Civilizations"** in it. <u>It holds only one culture and that is "obedience" to the Sustainer,</u> serving the trajectory and the purpose individually and collectively for which they all are created. This is the discipline and absolute destiny to which each is running fast and very accurately to fulfill the will of its Creator and Sustainer. **That is why there is complete peace and harmony everywhere in this universe, in complete contrast to human society where there is no justice and peace as humans are running their affairs as per their own <u>freewill</u> that the Supreme Master endowed each of them with as a paramount test of humans existence on earth as to whether they obey their Lord or deny His authority by exercising their free will in the correct or wrong way.**

This entire scenario of strict discipline, prevailing in this cosmos, is the essence of the physical world. It can be better understood from **Verse # 83 of Surah #3 Al-'Imran:**

أَفَغَيْرَ دِينِ اللَّهِ يَبْغُونَ وَلَهُ أَسْلَمَ مَنْ فِي السَّمَاوَاتِ وَالْأَرْضِ طَوْعًا وَكَرْهًا وَإِلَيْهِ يُرْجَعُونَ

"Do they seek, perchance, a system of life [Deen] other than of Allah, although it is unto Him that whatever is in the heavens

and on earth surrenders itself, willingly or unwillingly, and unto Him all must return."

* Special Guidance: This is for humans, the supreme creation of Allah and also for Jin who were created before man. Both are His willful creation. Man is the vicegerent of Allah on earth. Allah created man by His own hands and when Shaytan refused to bow down to Adam, He asked him:

قَالَ يَا إِبْلِيسُ مَا مَنَعَكَ أَنْ تَسْجُدَ لِمَا خَلَقْتُ بِيَدَيَّ أَسْتَكْبَرْتَ أَمْ كُنْتَ مِنَ الْعَالِينَ

"O Iblees (Shaytan)! What has kept you from prostrating yourself before [that] being which <u>I have created with My hands</u>? Are you too proud [to bow down before another created being] or are you of those who think [only] of themselves as high?"
[Qur'an, Surah SAD, 38:75]

Let us envision the scenario of man's creation and his coming to the earth with what mission to fulfill? This is the only way to understand why Guidance is his greatest need.

- Allah (SWT) Himself created man [Adam] and his wife from him with three strong urges and one freewill, as mentioned earlier;

- Allah then created this cosmos, heavens and earth, and harnessed it for the benefit of man for his exploration and use;

أَلَمْ تَرَوْا أَنَّ اللَّهَ سَخَّرَ لَكُمْ مَا فِي السَّمَاوَاتِ وَمَا فِي الْأَرْضِ وَأَسْبَغَ عَلَيْكُمْ نِعَمَهُ ظَاهِرَةً وَبَاطِنَةً

"Are you not aware that Allah has harnessed or made subservient to you all that it is in the heaven and all that is on earth and has lavished upon you His blessings, both outward and inward?"
[Qur'an, Surah Luqman, 31: 20]

اللَّهُ الَّذِي سَخَّرَ لَكُمُ الْبَحْرَ لِتَجْرِيَ الْفُلْكُ فِيهِ بِأَمْرِهِ وَلِتَبْتَغُوا مِنْ
فَضْلِهِ وَلَعَلَّكُمْ تَشْكُرُونَ
وَسَخَّرَ لَكُم مَّا فِي السَّمَاوَاتِ وَمَا فِي الْأَرْضِ جَمِيعًا مِّنْهُ

"It is Allah Who has made the ocean subservient unto you –so that ships might sail through it at His behest, and that you might seek to obtain [what you need] of His bounty and that you might have cause to be grateful.
And He has made subservient to you, [as a gift] from Himself, all that is in heaven and on earth ..."
[Qur'an, Surah Al- Jathiyah, 45: 12 -13]

Allah then brought forth the progenies of Adam, from their reins, their seeds, and made them testify of themselves (saying): "Am I not your Lord?" They said, "Yea, verily."

This entire scenario has been presented in the **Qur'an, Surah Al-A'raf, 7: 172]**

وَإِذْ أَخَذَ رَبُّكَ مِنْ بَنِي آدَمَ مِنْ ظُهُورِهِمْ ذُرِّيَّتَهُمْ وَأَشْهَدَهُمْ عَلَى
أَنْفُسِهِمْ أَلَسْتُ بِرَبِّكُمْ ۖ قَالُوا بَلَىٰ ۛ شَهِدْنَا ۚ أَنْ تَقُولُوا يَوْمَ الْقِيَامَةِ إِنَّا
كُنَّا عَنْ هَٰذَا غَافِلِينَ

"And (remember) when thy Sustainer brings forth offspring from the loins of the children of Adam, [He thus] call upon them to bear witness about themselves]: 'Am I not your Sustainer?' – [to which they answer]:' Yes indeed, we do bear witness thereto'. [Of this We remind you,] lest you say on the Day of Resurrection, 'Verily, we were unaware of this'."
[Qur'an, Surah Al- A'raf, 7: 172]

- And in the infinity of time, thy Sustainer said unto the angels: Behold: Lo! I am about to place a Khalifah (a Vicegerent) on earth and taught Adam all the names ['**Ilm** -knowledge of everything]. Then said unto the angels: "Prostrate yourselves before Adam."

They fell prostrate, all save **Iblees**. He refused to bow down before Adam out of arrogance and became an open enemy of Adam and his progenies till doomsday. Allah then directed both Adam and His wife to live in **Jannah** and enjoy all except one restriction: not to go near a particularly pinpointed tree. However, their arch enemy **Iblees** instigated them to eat from that prohibited tree. They disobeyed Allah. In consequence, their **"'Awrah"** (shame) was manifest, which they covered hurriedly with the leaves of trees in **Jannah**. Seeing this situation Allah addressed Adam: Have I told you not to go to that tree and warned you that **Iblees** is your open enemy. Adam and his wife immediately realized their mistake, repented and prayed to Allah,

قَالَا رَبَّنَا ظَلَمْنَا أَنْفُسَنَا وَإِنْ لَمْ تَغْفِرْ لَنَا وَتَرْحَمْنَا لَنَكُونَنَّ مِنَ الْخَاسِرِينَ

"Our Lord! We have wronged ourselves. If you forgive us not and have not mercy on us, surely we are of the lost!"
[Qur'an, Surah Al-A'raf, 7: 23]

Allah pardoned the mistakes of both Adam and his wife, and they had no burden to carry, like the "stigma of original sin" which was mistakenly propounded by Christianity. Allah (SWT) just said to them:
"You all go down to earth where you will receive My Guidance" (on how to live, act and behave on earth through My appointed Messengers.) ؟

فَتَلَقَّىٰ آدَمُ مِنْ رَبِّهِ كَلِمَاتٍ فَتَابَ عَلَيْهِ إِنَّهُ هُوَ التَّوَّابُ الرَّحِيمُ قُلْنَا اهْبِطُوا مِنْهَا جَمِيعًا فَإِمَّا يَأْتِيَنَّكُمْ مِنِّي هُدًى فَمَنْ تَبِعَ هُدَايَ فَلَا خَوْفٌ عَلَيْهِ وَلَا هُمْ يَحْزَنُونَ وَالَّذِينَ كَفَرُوا وَكَذَّبُوا بِآيَاتِنَا أُولَٰئِكَ أَصْحَابُ النَّارِ هُمْ فِيهَا خَالِدُونَ

Allah (SWT) ordains in these words:

"Thereupon Adam received words [of guidance] from his Sustainer, and He accepted his repentance: for, verily, He alone is the Acceptor of Repentance , the Dispenser of Grace, [And directed both], *Go down all of you from hence: but verily there comes unto you Guidance from Me: and those who follow My guidance need have no fear, and neither shall they grieve; but those who are bent on denying the truth and deny our revelation, such are rightful owners of the Fire. They will abide therein."*
Qur'an, Surah Al-Baqarah, 2: 37 -39]

This entire scenario that I have summarized above in brief is from Surah Al-Baqarah, 2: 30-39, and Surah Al-A'raf, 7:11-24, to ascertain that Allah (SWT) while ordering Adam to descend to earth "committed" Himself to continue sending Guidance to humans [Adam's progenies] as and when this Guidance would be lost, innovated or mutilated due to humans' interpolation and corruption of Divine Guidance, so that humans will not be able to say on the Day of Judgment that they had no Guidance at any time of their existence on earth as an excuse.

Allah (SWT) stood by His commitment to human beings. As such, there was no period when human society was ever living without Divine Guidance from their Lord delivered through His appointed Messengers from Adam, Noah, Abraham, David, Moses Jesus (and others) and the last Messenger Muhammad [May Allah be pleased with all of them].

Allah (SWT) maintained both the continuity of Prophethood in a chain and that of the Message - * Obedience to the Creator and Sustainer, * following the Messenger of the time as the model and *the accountability in Akhirah for all actions and deeds on earth. Prophet Muhammad (S) is the last prophet of Allah in the series and no Prophet was or is to come after him (S). After his (S) departure, his (S) followers, his (S) Ummah were and are to carry out that mission of Prophethood till the Day of Resurrection.

- Allah (SWT), in His infinite mercy, arranged this process of sending guidance to mankind **to meet human being's greatest need on earth. Why is it so? Why Guidance is human's Greatest Need? Can man live on earth without Divine Guidance? Can man deliver the Guidance by himself? With what consequences he will do it then? Is man competent to do so?** *Is man really desperate for Divine Guidance? And why is he/she always found begging for:* "<u>Ehdina Al-Sirat Al-Mustaqeem" – O Allah! Keep me, show me and guide me on straight path?</u> Let us discuss the nature behind this urgency.

WHY IS DIVINE GUIDANCE MAN'S GREATEST NEED?

As quoted earlier, Allah (SWT) created man and woman out of man with three strong urges and one free will, and descended them to earth as His vicegerent (**Khalifah**) for testing: **How does he live on earth? How does he utilize His enormous bounties** - the material environment created and harnessed for man? **And how does he use the personal trusts (Amanah) endowed to him/her** – time, talents, energies and resources - to the benefit of man and his society or otherwise? This paramount objective is clearly stated **by Allah in the following Verses:**

وَهُوَ الَّذِي خَلَقَ السَّمَاوَاتِ وَالْأَرْضَ فِي سِتَّةِ أَيَّامٍ وَكَانَ عَرْشُهُ عَلَى الْمَاءِ لِيَبْلُوَكُمْ أَيُّكُمْ أَحْسَنُ عَمَلًا

"And He it is Who created the heavens and earth in six days - and His Throne was upon the water – that He might try you, which of you is best in conduct."

[Qur'an, Surah HUD, 11: 7]

وَهُوَ الَّذِي جَعَلَكُمْ خَلَائِفَ الْأَرْضِ وَرَفَعَ بَعْضَكُمْ فَوْقَ بَعْضٍ دَرَجَاتٍ لِيَبْلُوَكُمْ فِ مَا آتَاكُمْ إِنَّ رَبَّكَ سَرِيعُ الْعِقَابِ وَإِنَّهُ لَغَفُورٌ رَحِيمٌ

"He it is who placed you as vicegerent on earth and has exalted some of you in rank above others that He may try you by (the test of) that which He had given you (bestowed upon you as Amanah - Trust). Lo! Thy Lord is swift in prosecution (in retribution): yet behold, He is indeed much-forgiving, a dispenser of grace (Merciful)."

[Qur'an, Al-An'am, 6: 165]

This situation brings us to the point: Is Divine Guidance really so important for man to live by on earth whereas his paramount basic needs of life are always found super-most in his mind while struggling for his existence on earth – food, unpolluted air, clean drinking water, a shelter and clothes to cover his body – the essentials for him to survive on earth?

This pertinent question brings us to some more realities of life. Is the Creator and Sustainer so callous that He descended man on earth and then left him to the vagaries of natural phenomenon, doing nothing for his survival, leaving the ever-lasting responsibility on man's shoulders, always to beg for His guidance and live only seeking His pleasure throughout his existence on earth? It would have been a far fledged supposition from the Creator and Sustainer of this cosmos to think even for a moment that when He provides **"RIZQ" (provision)**, covering all the physical needs of man and other animate objects of this universe, how   could He ignore arrangement for the moral and spiritual needs of man on earth. The **Qur'an** confirms categorically and elaborates how He fulfils all and every need of man on earth. **Let us deal first with man's physical needs and see how He fulfills them.**

وَكَأَيِّنْ مِنْ دَابَّةٍ لَا تَحْمِلُ رِزْقَهَا اللَّهُ يَرْزُقُهَا وَإِيَّاكُمْ ۚ وَهُوَ السَّمِيعُ الْعَلِيمُ

"And how many a living creature is there that takes no thought of its own sustenance, [the while] God provides it as [He provides] for you – since He alone is all-hearing all-knowing."

[Qur'an, Al-Ankabut, 29: 60]

See His magnanimity in providing the basic needs of man and other living species.

*AIR: It is available in abundance at every place on earth. Where there is a vacuum, the place is empty, and air moves in and fills the place. Allah has disciplined nature with the principle of filling the gap where it is empty as man cannot live without air even for a couple of minutes. He has arranged this natural phenomenon to work to this effect. We exhale carbon dioxide which is absorbed constantly by trees and plants as their need to survive, in turn producing oxygen in a continuous process that humans inhale to live on earth. That is why human society has to do a lot of forestation and reforestation beside the natural forests around the world. Allah meets this basic need of man totally free of any charge, but it is man who is spoiling the purity of AIR and poisoning it through pollution of the atmosphere in all the big cities by ever-increasing the pace of industrialization and heavy transportation on land, air and sea.

* WATER": Water like air is also a great need of man. Man cannot survive without it for more than a couple of days. It is available in abundance though drinking water is limited to only 0.9 % of the total water on earth. The water in seas and oceans and water that is stored on mountain tops around the world are the big reservoirs of fresh water. From oceans it evaporates into vapors with the heat of the sun, especially in doldrums areas, goes up into the sky where condensation takes place, air and winds move it to different parts of the world **under His commands** and falls in the shape of rain and ice on the mountains in its most distilled form in places and regions **as Allah ordains to meet human needs on earth**. The heat of the sun melts the snow at mountain tops and glaciers, water flows in rivers down in the valleys, plains and deltas for irrigation and other human consumption. Allah (SWT) has arranged this system to work most efficiently through the two huge reservoirs of water at sea and ice on mountain tops. The system has been busy meeting human needs and urgencies for water constantly round the year since the time earth was created and made habitable for man billions of years ago..

However, man is polluting these sources of pure water with huge amounts of chemicals and contaminated used water coming out of huge industrial complexes that are dumped every day in the natural sources of water, making it impossible for humans, especially those in the poor and underdeveloped countries of Asia, Africa and Latin America to get enough pure drinking water for their natural needs. **Man has polluted both air and water** that He created and arranged for living species on earth. **However, the sources of both the physical necessities of man are available in abundance, more than the human needs all around the world. Man has to learn only how to use them without damaging the purity of natural sources.**

* **RIZQ – PROVISION:** Food is equally an important basic need of man to live and survive on earth. A human being cannot survive without food, be healthy, energetic and productive after a couple of weeks if it is denied to him. Food, air and water provide the basic ingredients to the body to maintain itself in the service of self, family and the society at large. Allah made a broad based arrangement to meet this paramount need of man everywhere and at every place. He ordains:

وَلَقَدْ مَكَّنَّاكُمْ فِي الْأَرْضِ وَجَعَلْنَا لَكُمْ فِيهَا مَعَايِشَ ۗ قَلِيلًا مَا تَشْكُرُونَ

"Yea, Indeed, [O men] We have given you a [bountiful] place on earth and appointed thereon means of livelihood for you: [yet] how seldom are you grateful!"
[Qur'an, Surah Al-A'raf, 7: 10]

وَآتَاكُمْ مِنْ كُلِّ مَا سَأَلْتُمُوهُ ۚ وَإِنْ تَعُدُّوا نِعْمَتَ اللَّهِ لَا تُحْصُوهَا ۗ إِنَّ الْإِنْسَانَ لَظَلُومٌ كَفَّارٌ

"And He gives you all you ask of Him (He generously meets all human needs and urgencies, proving that your creator arranged every thing for your needs), and if you count the bounties of Allah you cannot reckon it. Lo! Man is verily a wrong-doer, an ingrate."
[Qur'an, Surah Ibrahim, 14: 34]

However, for getting **"Rizq"** (Provision), Allah (SWT) has attached two important conditions to fulfill in order to obtain food or provision on earth. It is not free like air and water. For arranging food on the dinner table, a lot of human labor is required at different stages to make it affordable and eatable. Man can and cannot use it in its raw and natural shape as air and water can be. The land is there to plough it to grow food items; the water is there to irrigate the land, the sun is there to make the crop ripe and harvestable, the transport system is there to move it to market places making it accessible to man to fill his stomach. This entire process is subject to human efforts. That is why Allah (SWT) has ordained man to fulfill the two conditions as stated below:

1, **Verse # 39 & 40 of Surah # 53: Al-Najm:**

وَأَنْ لَيْسَ لِلْإِنْسَانِ إِلَّا مَا سَعَىٰ - وَأَنَّ سَعْيَهُ سَوْفَ يُرَىٰ

"And that man has only that for which he makes efforts [in every field of life]; And that in time [the nature of] all his striving will be shown [to him]."

2. **Verse # 26 & 27 of Al-'Imran:**

The Rizq is given by Allah in His own estimation: some may get in abundance whereas some may get a little, as He ordains in Verse # 26 and 27 of Al-'Imran wherein Allah describes His prerogatives in controlling and managing the affairs of this world, including the distribution of Rizq:

قُلِ اللَّهُمَّ مَالِكَ الْمُلْكِ تُؤْتِي الْمُلْكَ مَنْ تَشَاءُ وَتَنْزِعُ الْمُلْكَ مِمَّنْ تَشَاءُ وَتُعِزُّ مَنْ تَشَاءُ وَتُذِلُّ مَنْ تَشَاءُ بِيَدِكَ الْخَيْرُ إِنَّكَ عَلَى كُلِّ شَيْءٍ قَدِيرٌ

تُولِجُ اللَّيْلَ فِي النَّهَارِ وَتُولِجُ النَّهَارَ فِي اللَّيْلِ وَتُخْرِجُ الْحَيَّ مِنَ الْمَيِّتِ وَتُخْرِجُ الْمَيِّتَ مِنَ الْحَيِّ وَتَرْزُقُ مَنْ تَشَاءُ بِغَيْرِ حِسَابٍ

"Say: "O Allah! Lord of all domination! You grant domination unto whom You will, and take away domination from whom You will; and You exalt who You will, and abase whom You will. In Your hand is all good. Verily, You have the power to do anything.

You make the night grow longer by shortening the day, and You make the day grow longer by shortening the night. And You bring forth the living out of that which is dead, and You bring forth the dead out of that which is alive. And You grant sustenance unto whom Thou will, beyond all reckoning."
[Qur'an, Al-'Imran, 3: 26 -27]

3. ALLAH'S UNSDERTAKING TOWARDS HUMAN'S RIZQ:

It is clearly pronounced in Verses # 56 – 58 of Surah # 51: Al-Dhariyat:

وَمَا خَلَقْتُ الْجِنَّ وَالْإِنْسَ إِلَّا لِيَعْبُدُونَ
مَا أُرِيدُ مِنْهُمْ مِنْ رِزْقٍ وَمَا أُرِيدُ أَنْ يُطْعِمُونَ
إِنَّ اللَّهَ هُوَ الرَّزَّاقُ ذُو الْقُوَّةِ الْمَتِينُ

"I created the Jin and humankind only that they might worship Me; I seek no livelihood from them, nor do I ask that they should feed Me;

For, verily, Allah Himself is the provider of all sustenance, the Lord of all might, the Eternal."
The above quotes form the Qur'an show that when Allah Himself has taken care of providing the physical necessities of humans, like air and water in abundance, and food with two natural conditions, these ingredients could not constitute man's greatest need on earth. Man would get and meet his basic needs one way or the other. He can fulfill his **physical needs and urgencies** by struggling hard and sometimes easily from the environment where he lives, **depending upon the system that controls it**. The question arises: How and from where will he meet the demands of his **moral life, its needs and urgencies, as how to act, live and behave on earth? Is he to live like a responsible human being or a reckless creature? Is the worldly life the only life of man? Is it going to end one day with no consequences of his good or bad deeds for him to bear?**

Will it not be a great injustice if I don't get any reward for my good deeds or any punishment for my evil deeds? I don't think the case is like that. **I think that I must have some definite Guidance on how to live, act and behave on earth, and perhaps that is my greatest need. What I feel and see is that in the absence of proper Guidance humans become reckless and are filling the earth with chaos, confusion, bloodshed and total disorder in every walk of life.**

Now, from where can man get that guidance? Can he develop it on his own accord or can he get it from humans like me? Let us examine its implications. Can man do it, and what happened to the efforts he has made so far to satisfy this greatest need of man?

4. CAN MAN DELIVER THE GUIDANCE?

To fulfill this greatest need of man, human beings have always been trying in the past and are trying today, too, to deliver a system of life for man to live on earth in peace. History presents a scenario of such human efforts since time immemorial, but with what results? **All failed miserably as man is not competent at all to**

frame or deliver a system for his species due to the following reasons:

- **Due to lack of knowledge** of the past, which very often lies in obscurity; of the present, which may not be comprehensive at all; and of the future that is totally unknown to him even for a second onward;

- **Due to his inability** to surmount and comprehend all the needs and problems of human society of every part and region of the globe and the people living therein;

- **Due to his temperament** and human nature which leans toward greed, partiality, favoritism, personal likes and dislikes, hatred and animosity to others, racial, language and class discrimination or prejudices within the human society together with the growing corporate interests and urge for economic domination where exploitation of the poor and the needy is dominant;

- These shortcomings, urges and tendencies were always there in humans and hence man failed to deliver any system of life in the past throughout the ages and has bitterly failed today in the modern age of enlightenment. **The failure of tribalism, feudalism, communism, socialism, fascism and capitalism; all are before the ken of our mortal eyes.** Human history establishes the hopelessness of man's effort in very deplorable words. The whole saga of kings and queens, the Cold War in between East and West, present-day inherent growing doubts and apprehensions about Globalization, the Market Economy and WTO (the World Trade Organization) must open our eyes that man, due to his enormous shortcomings, cannot succeed in the onerous task of delivering a perfect system of life for mankind in order to live in peace and harmony on earth. **Man proved by his own efforts that he is just incompetent to do it, either by establishing the Dictatorship of the Proletariat or by rendering the people as sovereign in capitalistic societies**. Both are at opposite ends of the pole and operating at extremes against human nature. So is the case of modern liberal democracies and socialistic capitalism around the world. **Humanity was and is crying with pain and agony under each man-made system.**

This reminded me of a speech given in early 1956 by the Late Choudhry Ali Ahmad Khan Marhum, the then Amir of Jamaat-i-Islami, East Pakistan [BD], when he was delivering a lecture on the comparative study of Communism, Capitalism and Islam in District Board Hall, Dacca. He put the comparison like this: Capitalism puts humans to stand on head, guaranteeing all human liberties and freedom but no guarantee to fill the stomach; Communism, in turn, puts the humanity to stand on stomach, guaranteeing employment for everyone [that is food for the belly] but no guarantee for liberty and freedom; whereas Islam keeps the man to stand erect on his legs and guarantees meeting the demands both of mind and stomach. It was the most appropriate comparison of the three competitive Isms. The audience loved this comparison and it was the talk of the town for a long time. Fortunately, I was present in that intellective gathering which was attended by a lot of learned scholars of the city.

It has brought us to the point **to acknowledge the failure of man to deliver the guidance, a system of life showing how to lead a life of peace on earth, due to inherent shortcomings of man The question arises: Who, then, can deliver the guidance to man to lead a life of justice, peace and harmony on earth, with complete assurance and guarantees that there will be no exploitation or discrimination of any kind at any stage of human life, with complete freedom and all liberties of mind and faculties of heart.** Let us attend to the most pertinent question of our existence on earth: **From where to get the Guidance?**

5. THE ONLY AUTHORITY:

At this juncture man has no choice but to turn his face to his Creator and Sustainer for seeking Guidance from Him and he implores Him: **"EHDINA AL-Sirat-AL-MUSTAQEEM" [Keep us and guide us on straight path – "Sirat-AL -MUSTAQEEM" as it**

stands now as his Greatest Need on earth. It is not air, water or food, and at the same time none on earth could deliver it in any from or shape. Man, thus, cuts a very sorry figure in his constant failure to deliver the guidance, a balanced system of life, to his species to live in peace and order on earth... **He comes to the conclusion:**

Allah is our Creator and Sustainer. He knows our shortcomings, our strengths and weaknesses, our needs and urges to their minutest details. He knows the past, the present, and is totally well aware of the future in all respects. His authority is Supreme, indivisible and inalienable and his prerogatives are limitless all-surmounting, as we have seen in Verse # 255 of Al-Baqarah and Verses # 26 and 27 of Al-'Imran. He knows what is in our hearts and minds, and He knows our destiny which is an integral part of His limitless "'ILM" (knowledge). He knows what would be good for humanity both at individual and collective levels and what would be bad.

The entire cosmos and what it contains are in His hands and He can do and undo things just by saying: "Kun! Fa-yakun" [Be! and it is there.]. He loves human beings and gives provision to whom he wishes in abundance at His discretion even to His arch enemies and disbelievers indiscriminately. He is just in granting the amenities of life to all and sundry with no distinction. It is He Who has the right and authority to deliver the Guidance to mankind, especially when He is "committed" or has undertaken to do so when He ordained Adam to go down on earth, and He will continue to send Guidance to mankind, as and when it will lose it due to human mutilation or innovations.
        "He is always nearer to us than our jugular veins..."
            [Qur'an, Surah Qaf: 50: 16]

وَنَحْنُ أَقْرَبُ إِلَيْهِ مِنْ حَبْلِ الْوَرِيد

"And He is always with His ''Abd' (servant) wherever he is...."
            [Qur'an, Surah Al-Hadeed, 57: 4]

وَهُوَ مَعَكُمْ أَيْنَ مَا كُنْتُم

As such, none can be so highly informed about me, my needs and urgencies than my Creator and Sustainer. Equally, none is so much competent and perfect to fulfill my greatest need on earth as my Lord is, regarding how to live, act and behave on earth in total peace and harmony with my fellow human beings. So, man prays to his Sustainer to keep him on the Straight Path ["Sirat Al-Mustaqeem"] during Salah and out of Salah as this is man's Greatest Need and as man cannot live without that. A Muslim has complete confidence that the Creator and Sustainer is ever responding to his humble calls and showers His blessings upon him incessantly, if he sincerely submits and supplicates to Him.

At this juncture His slave wants to be sure that his prayers for Guidance are granted and that no anomalous situation is left. His "'Abd" [slave] immediately qualifies his prayers by adding or elucidating his prayers with these qualifying words:

صِرَاطَ الَّذِينَ أَنْعَمْتَ عَلَيْهِمْ غَيْرِ الْمَغْضُوبِ عَلَيْهِمْ وَلَا الضَّالِّينَ

"THE STRAIGHT PATH OF THOSE WHOM YOU REWARDED, not (the path) of those who go astray. "

Let us examine the logical dimensions of this qualification as to what it foretells:

The outright qualification of man for guidance deals with two important aspects of man's behavior or treatment of the Guidance from his Sustainer. Guidance has been coming to man in a chain as and when it was lost due to human innovations or textual mutilations. Either the people accepted the guidance and followed it, or denied it and rejected the Prophet of the time. So, these two attitudes of acceptance or of denial and rejection are operating in human society side by side since the coming of Adam and Eve on earth. Those who accepted the guidance and led the life as Allah ordained were rewarded by the Supreme Lord with exalted positions, and those who refused the guidance and followed their own path of worldly pursuits, they stand condemned throughout human history.

Thus, we have to evaluate separately the treatment of both altitudes, which are of those individuals who were glorified by Allah in their quest to seek His pleasure, distinctly identifiable from those who lost the guidance that came from their Lord. Al-Fatiha clearly illustrates these two characters of human society that have always been living together in our midst. Each carries very visible signs of distinction, demonstrating clearly who the blessed ones are and who the condemned ones are.

CHAPTER - 4

VII. HOW HUMANS TREATED THE GUIDANCE?

The Attitude of acceptance or rejection:

A. THE ATTITUDE OF ACCEPTANCE:

"Sirat ALLADHINA AN'AMTA 'ALAYHIM": The Path of those whom You have favored or rewarded" – The Attitude of Acceptance:

It might be extremely difficult to know through our human estimation who are the individuals or the people whom Allah has rewarded, who stand qualified for His glorification and decoration, or who have fulfilled the objective of their life on earth in attaining the pleasure of their Lord and have not lost that golden opportunity through their own ignorance, obstinacy or falling in love with the path that was prohibited by their Lord. Out of His infinite mercy, Allah (SWT) has enlisted the people of the highest cadre whom He rewarded immensely. He placed them with the highest profile of human deeds and actions on earth in carrying out their life-long struggle towards establishing His authority on self, family and the society. They were living to the extent that they sacrificed all that He endowed them with – time, life, talents and resources – all to attain His pleasure in order to establish *justice* ('Adl wa Qist) in the abode of man and in every walk of life. That list of approved and rewarded dignitaries is given in **Verse # 69 & 70 of Surah # 4: Al-Nisa:**

وَمَنْ يُطِعِ اللَّهَ وَالرَّسُولَ فَأُولَٰئِكَ مَعَ الَّذِينَ أَنْعَمَ اللَّهُ عَلَيْهِمْ مِنَ النَّبِيِّينَ وَالصِّدِّيقِينَ وَالشُّهَدَاءِ وَالصَّالِحِينَ ۚ وَحَسُنَ أُولَٰئِكَ رَفِيقًا ذَٰلِكَ الْفَضْلُ مِنَ اللَّهِ ۚ وَكَفَىٰ بِاللَّهِ عَلِيمًا

"For all those who obey Allah [pay heed unto God] and the Messenger shall be among those upon whom Allah has

bestowed His blessings [God has shown favor]: the <u>Prophets,</u>
and [those who never deviated from the truth,[the path of
righteousness] – <u>Al-Siddiqeen</u>; the martyrs – [those who bore
witness to the truth by sacrificing their lives in the way of
Allah] – <u>Al-Shuhadah</u>] and [the righteous ones] <u>Al- Saleheen</u>:
and how Godly a company are these! Such is the bounty of
Allah –and none has the knowledge which Allah has."
<u>*[Qur'an, Surah Al-Nisa, 4: 69 -70]*</u>

Out of these four approved categories, Prophets are not coming any more. Prophet Muhammad (S) was the last Messenger of Allah appointed on earth for the guidance of mankind. The **Muslim Ummah now stands in the witness box of history to call the humanity to the fold of its Creator and Sustainer exactly on the lines Rasulullah (S) did. His (S) life pattern is now the perfect model for Muslims till the Doomsday.** But the other three categories of distinction: **Al-Siddiqeen, Al- Shuhadah and Al-Saleheen** are wide open for all of us to try to attain. They all will be in heaven in the company of Prophets, enjoying the endless bounties of Allah.

It sets the ideal for Muslims to struggle for the whole of their life towards the attainment of these distinctive positions with Allah (SWT). It is not a difficult task at all. Allah's Guidance in the shape of the **Qur'an** is totally intact in our hands in its most original and perfect form and its inspiring model too is available within the life pattern of Rasulullah (S) in its minutest details in most accomplished form. We are not to grapple in darkness like the Jews and the Christians who have practically lost their books of guidance and are holding only some dogmas and stories and that, too, in the most dilapidated condition. They even could not implement the Ten Commandments of the Torah anywhere in the world of Christendom. The Muslims are the most fortunate in this respect as **Allah Himself undertook the onerous task of protection and preservation of the complete text of Guidance intact in its original words and contents in which the Qur'an was revealed to Prophet Muhammad (S) to this day and till Qiyamah (<u>The</u>**

Day of judgment). Allah describes this undertaking in **Verse # 9 of Surah # 15: Al-Hijr:**

$$\text{إِنَّا نَحْنُ نَزَّلْنَا الذِّكْرَ وَإِنَّا لَهُ لَحَافِظُونَ}$$

"Behold, it is We Ourselves who have bestowed from on high, step by step, this Reminder [the Qur'an] and, behold, it is We who shall truly guard it [from all corruption]."

[Qur'an, Surah Al-Hijr, 15: 9]

Every Muslim and Muslimah on earth by reciting **Kalimah** (The Word), **La Ilaha Ilallah** commits himself/herself to uphold it under each and every circumstance, to live and die for His Deen and undertake to struggle for the whole of his/her life for the **Iqamah of Allah's Deen** on this earth. In this process he/she tries his/her best always to live like a truthful, conscientious Muslim and Muslimah, demonstrate the moral behavior that Allah loves, perform the affairs of his/her life on the pattern Allah ordains, deal with his/her fellow humans with love, care, and concern, render humanitarian services to neighbors and fellow citizens, spend his/her wealth for the betterment of the life of the have-nots and, equally, cements his/her relations with Allah (SWT) as His " **'Abd**".. In short, a Muslim always tries his utmost to **"be good and do good to others,"** presenting total devotion, love and dedication to Allah and serving humanity with good deeds (**'Amalus-Salih**), **In fact, his good deeds are the truthful reflection of his Iman** .The stronger the Iman, the greater will be the quantum of his good deeds. Both Iman and good deeds go together. It would be next to impossible to have good deeds without having perfect **Iman**.

Now, if a strong Iman in Allah is there and it is handsomely reflected in one's good deeds in the society in which he lives, he cannot keep himself aloof from his assignment from Allah to call the people of the land, his countrymen and women, to His fold, thereby making every possible effort to change the society in due course of time through the peaceful process of Dawah Ilallah towards establishing His Deen in place of the prevailing Godless creeds, rooting out what is prohibited (Munkar) and advocating what is Ma'ruf (eternal truth). However, the struggle for Iqamah of Allah's Deen would never be acceptable to our adversaries and the vested interests of the time. It would be opposed tooth and nail at every step, causing very often extreme hardship to the Da'ee. It is inevitable and the Da'ee has to bear the brunt of hardship with "Sabr and Hikmah" [patience and wisdom], while always begging Nusrah (help) from Allah in this life- long pursuit.

Allah (SWT) has ordained this entire process of **Iman**, good deeds, struggle for Allah's Deen and sustaining the onslaughts of the Evil forces in a sequence in **Surah # 103: Al-ASR:**

وَالْعَصرِ — إِنَّ الْإِنْسَانَ لَفِي خُسْرٍ
إِلَّا الَّذِينَ آمَنُوا وَعَمِلُوا الصَّالِحَاتِ وَتَوَاصَوْا بِالْحَقّ وَتَوَاصَوْا
بِالصَّبْرِ

"Consider the flight of time! Verily, man is bound to lose himself, unless he be of those who attain to faith, and do good works and enjoin [exhort] upon one another the keeping to truth and enjoin [exhort] upon one another patience in adversity."
[Qur'an, Al-Asr, 103: 1 -3]

EVALUATION OF SURAH Al-ASR:

This small Surah is extremely important, as in the words Imam Sha'fii (RA), **"Had Allah revealed only Surah Al-Asr [for the guidance of the people] it would have been sufficient for them, had they just pondered over its contents [as what it demands and what they are to do]."** It has four comprehensive meaningful phrases:

It categorically exerts that the entire humanity is lost except those who have:

1.   Iman (faith in Allah): Here, "Iman" is used in its total (Mutlaq) sense;
2. And do good deeds –" Wa 'Amal-us-Salihat";
3. And (do) "Tawasaw Bil-Haq" [exhort one another to stand by truth and its advocacy];
4. And (do) "Tawasaw Bis-SAbr" [exhort one another to have patience when trials and adversities are encountered in its wake].

- In fact, this is the essence of **Deen–Al-Islam**. When one who has become Muslim has faith in Allah **(Iman Billah)**, he consciously commits himself to obey Allah alone, follows His directives meticulously in every walk of life, keeps away from what is wrong (Munkar), calls the people to the fold of the Creator and Sustainer as the topmost priority of his life, and puts all his time, talents, energies and resources into establishing His authority on self, family and the society while he is constantly involved in doing, practicing and promoting good deeds.

- In fact, "Wa 'Amal-us-Salihat"- good deeds that a **Mu'min** performs are the **logical demands and effects** of his **Iman** in Allah. As such, the quantum of his good deeds is endless. It covers the entire spectrum of his life-long activities both in personal and collective spheres - from birth to death and from cradle to grave. It covers the total range of individual **'Ebadah**, moral codes of conduct, man's entire socio-economic-political affairs, with constant deep involvement in calling people to the fold of Allah, making all possible efforts to eradicate evils from the society while doing his utmost to establish the **Ma'ruf** by spending his time, talents, energies and resources in its wake all around.

This all comes within the domain of "'Amal-us-Salihat" (good deeds) and constitutes the integral part of his struggle for the Iqamah of Allah's Deen in its utmost form. The process of doing **'Amal-us-Salih" is the culminating point of Iman Billah**. This is the logical demand of believing in Allah. **Good deeds are the test of Iman Billah. If the good deeds as listed above do**

not follow in sequence, then that Iman is unproductive or not trust-worthy.

- **"Tawasaw Bil-Haq "**, exhorting one another to advocate for Truth, the **Deen** of Allah, in fact, is the essence of **Dawah Ilallah (inviting to the fold of Allah)**. An individual, howsoever he may be truthful and sincere in his commitment to Allah, cannot single-handedly fight against the prevalent evils in the society, establish **Ma'ruf (good)** in place of **Munkar (wrong)** and practice the **Deen** of Allah in every aspect of human life, both at individual and collective levels, unless he approaches his like-minded brothers and sisters and exhorts them to be his companions and **do the same "job" at each others' individual and collective levels**. Through this process of exhortation, a **Mu'min** galvanizes society to be actively involved collectively in **Dawah Ilallah** to get it changed and prepared towards the implementation of the Islamic system in every aspect of life. **"Tawasaw Bil-Haq"** is, thus, the most perfect, appropriate and effective mechanism **that Allah (SWT) has recommended and made obligatory on every Muslim and Muslimah to resort to as an integral part of his/her Iman and doing 'Amal-us-Saleh. His/her Iman and "'Amal-us-Saleh" will never achieve perfection if he/she is not actively involved in resorting to "Tawasaw Bil-Haq" as a regular and continuous feature of his/her life.**

This is Dawah Ilallah, a process towards involving the entire Muslim society in this onerous task to get the **Falah (the success)** in both the worlds. If they don't do this job as the most natural and logical demand of their **Iman**, they all will face **Khusran (the loss)** in both the worlds, as Allah assertively proclaims in this Surah at the very outset that: **Lo! Man is in a state of loss [Inna Al-Insana la-fi Khusr]**. The Muslim **Ummah** has to assess its position and see what Allah exhorts them to do. **Are they undertaking this task?** If not, they have to realize that in neglecting such a tremendous responsibility of their **Iman**, they stand nowhere in the community of nations and, hence, they must understand that it is in consequence of that neglect they are encountering only ignominy and disgrace everywhere in this world. **The beloved companions of Rasulullah (S) were always reminding each other about their responsibility in respect of Dawah Ilallah by reciting Surah Al-Asr when meeting together and when departing as the routine of their life. When they were doing this job of <u>"Tawasaw Bil-Haq"</u>, their adversaries had respect for them everywhere. We have neglected and are neglecting that job, and, consequently we are facing only disgrace everywhere. Will the Muslim Ummah and its leadership learn a lesson from this clarion call of their Lord, or will they prefer to "sleep" in the midst of the luxuries of the worldly life and in disgrace, especially in the West?**

7 RAKAT تكبير

Do the Muslims not pray at least <u>17</u> times a day in their obligatory Salah and seek Hidayah [Guidance] from their Lord, qualify their beseeching simultaneously by adding the <u>Sirat</u> (Path) of those who have been rewarded by Allah (<u>"Unamta 'Alayhim"</u>) – the path of those who are busy day in and day out in calling the humanity to the fold of their Creator and Sustainer. This is the logical demand of their Iman in Allah, resorting to good deeds and doing <u>"Tawasaw-Bil-Haq"</u>. <u>It is they who are "Al-Siddiqeen," "Al-Shuhadah" and "Al-Saleheen," as distinguished by Allah in Verse # 69, Surah # 4, Surah Al-Nisa, quoted above?</u>

- **<u>"Tawasaw Bis-Sabr,"</u>** <u>"exhorting one another to endurance,"</u> to have patience, in fact, is the climax of the long process of **Dawah Ilallah**. It needs some elaboration. The **Batil** of the time of Rasulullah (S) could not tolerate his (S) call of **Dawah Ilallah**. Similarly, the die-hard **Batil** of the "enlightened" societies of the modern age will react in the same way. The **Haqq** was never accepted in the past nor will it be accepted today or in the future. The fundamentals, both of **Haqq and Batil**, are quite different, totally antagonistic to each other. The Shaytanic forces of the time have opposed and will oppose tooth and nail against establishing the sovereignty of Allah on earth, a challenge thrown at Allah when

Iblees (Shaytan) refused to bow down to Adam out of arrogance and said to Allah that he [Shaytan] will sit in His straight path and instigate the people not to worship Him. This dialogue between Allah and Shaytan is vividly presented in **Surah Al-A'raf** and is worth studying to understand why the Shaytanic forces will never accept the truth easily. **On the refusal of Shaytan to bow down to Adam, Allah asked him, "What made you disobey My orders to prostrate?" Shaytan responded:**

قَالَ مَا مَنَعَكَ أَلَّا تَسْجُدَ إِذْ أَمَرْتُكَ ۖ قَالَ أَنَا خَيْرٌ مِنْهُ خَلَقْتَنِي مِنْ نَارٍ وَخَلَقْتَهُ مِنْ طِينٍ

قَالَ فَاهْبِطْ مِنْهَا فَمَا يَكُونُ لَكَ أَنْ تَتَكَبَّرَ فِيهَا فَاخْرُجْ إِنَّكَ مِنَ الصَّاغِرِينَ

قَالَ أَنْظِرْنِي إِلَىٰ يَوْمِ يُبْعَثُونَ – قَالَ إِنَّكَ مِنَ الْمُنْظَرِينَ

قَالَ فَبِمَا أَغْوَيْتَنِي لَأَقْعُدَنَّ لَهُمْ صِرَاطَكَ الْمُسْتَقِيمَ

ثُمَّ لَآتِيَنَّهُمْ مِنْ بَيْنِ أَيْدِيهِمْ وَمِنْ خَلْفِهِمْ وَعَنْ أَيْمَانِهِمْ وَعَنْ شَمَائِلِهِمْ ۖ وَلَا تَجِدُ أَكْثَرَهُمْ شَاكِرِينَ

قَالَ اخْرُجْ مِنْهَا مَذْءُومًا مَدْحُورًا ۖ لَمَنْ تَبِعَكَ مِنْهُمْ لَأَمْلَأَنَّ جَهَنَّمَ مِنْكُمْ أَجْمَعِينَ

"I am better than him (Adam). You created me of fire while him You did create of mud."
Then Allah said, "Then go down hence [from Jannah]! It is not for you to show pride here, so go forth! Lo! Thou are of those degraded."
He [Shaytan] said, "Reprieve me till the day when they are raised (from the dead)."
Allah Said, "Lo! You are of those reprieved."
(Then) Shaytan responded: " Now because You have sent me astray, verily, <u>I shall lurk in ambush for them on Your Right Path.</u> Then I shall come upon them from before and from behind them and from their right hands and from their left hands, and You will not find most of them grateful unto You."

(In response) He (Allah) said, "Go forth from hence, degraded, banished. As for such of them as follow you, surely I will fill hell with all of you."

[Qur'an, Surah Al-A'raf. 7: 12 -18]

This open dialogue of Shaytan with Allah (SWT) confirms once and for all that the believers in Allah, the followers of the Truth, calling the humanity to His fold will always be opposed on earth tooth and nail by the Shaytanic forces with no respite. The forces of **Haqq** will never be accepted to act freely for the spread of Allah's authority, His **Deen** unopposed. '**Allamah Iqbal** rightly and beautifully summed up the whole process of the inherent struggle between the forces of **Haqq** and **Batil** in this couplet:

"Satezakar raha hai azal sey ta imroze <> Chiraghe Mustafavi wa Shararey Bu-lahabi Ast"
[Translation: From the dawn of humanity to this day, the light of the lamp of Prophet Muhammad (S) has been fighting with the flames of Abu Lahab, the arch enemy of Islam, who struggled to his last breath to extinguish the light of Islam.]

The eternal episode between **Haqq and Batil** (Evil forces) presents the panoramic view of opposition of **Haqq** by **Batil**, a challenge of will of the followers of both the camps. As such, the opposition to Islamic forces is inevitable **when there is an organized effort** to introduce, spread and establish the **Deen** of Allah as a political entity on earth. When Allah (SWT) entrusted the **task of "Tawasaw Bil- Haq",** and concluded this **Surah** with an everlasting reminder to do **"Tawasaw Bis-SAbr"**, exhorting one another to endure the opposition, its hardship and inevitable trials and tribulations on this path.

Allah (SWT), thus, prepares **His team of Da'ees** right from the **very outset of the mission of Dawah Ilallah to be ready to bear these onslaughts of Shaytanic forces. Dawah efforts are not a bed of roses but of stiff thorns that Shaytanic forces will strew on the path of righteousness. Those who come out successful**

in this test will be rewarded the decoration prize of: Al-Siddiqeen and Al- Saleheen who live in the vicinity of Allah with His eternal bliss.

- Al- Shuhadah: It is another special distinguished qualification or position, and the most coveted award from Allah (SWT) for those who in the process of continuous struggle for the **Iqamah** (establishment) of His **Deen** at all the fronts – self, family, society and humanity at large, confronting the evil designs of **Batil** to crush the forces of **Haqq** through armed opposition, give up their life in this pursuit and become martyrs **- Shuhadah in the way of Allah**. They fulfill the demand of their **Iman**, the commitment to Allah, proving beyond any shadow of doubt that:

قُلْ إِنَّ صَلَاتِي وَنُسُكِي وَمَحْيَايَ وَمَمَاتِي لِلَّهِ رَبِّ الْعَالَمِينَ

[Qul Inna Salati, wa Nusuki, wa Mahyaya wa Mamati Lillahey Rabbil A'lameen."]

"Say: My Salah (worship) and my sacrifice, and my life, and my death are for Allah (SWT), the Sustainer of this cosmos:
[Qur'an, Surah Al-An'am, 6: 162]

This is the highest and the most glorious demonstration of **Iman** of a **Mu'min** to attain the coveted position of **"Shuhadah-Ala-Annas"** [**Witness to mankind**]. A Shaheed in the way of Allah fulfils his commitment to Allah by sacrificing his life and everything that he possesses for **His pleasure**. He, thus, joins the company of **"Al-Nabiyyeen, Al-Siddiqeen and Al-Saleheen"** in **Jannah** and they would be his best companions.

In fact, the above quoted **Verse** from **Surah Al-An'am** is one of the capsule **verses** (**Ayah**) of the **Qur'an**, presenting the essence of **Iman** and Islam – **total surrender to Allah** – in a few words in the most comprehensive way as discussed earlier about the **Verse**: **"Iyyaka Na'budu wa Iyyaka Nasta'een."** It exhorts each and every believer in Allah to assess his life in a continuous process and **see how he/she behaves on earth in cementing his relation with**

Allah on one hand and on the other with the suffering humanity at large, the have-nots.

It is, thus, clear that the successful **Mu'min** are only those who remain steadfast on "**Sirat Al- Mustaqeem**" and follow the path shown by **Al-Siddiqeen and Al-Saleheen** and are awarded the coveted prize of **Al-Shuhadah 'al-Annas"** by sacrificing everything in glorifying the authority of Allah. **There is no other way to be included in these cherished categories of Allah's approved list of slaves ('Abd) except struggling consciously towards the Iqamah of His Deen. Dawah Ilallah is the means and the process to that end to reach the milestones earmarked by Allah to attain after death in Verse # 69 of Surah Al-Nisa.**

A Muslim, therefore, when he reaches "**Unamta 'Alayhim"** while reciting Surah **Al-Fatiha** must beg from Allah (SWT) immediately in his heart: **O Allah! Include me in the finest category of those whom You have blessed from amongst: Al-Nabieen wa Al-Siddiqeen wa Al-Shuhadah wa Al-Saleheen.** And you know Allah's response comes immediately.

About this special blessing of Allah, I will discuss later by sharing a Hadith Qudsi narrated by Abu Hurairah (RA) and quoted by **Sahih Muslim.**

Dawah Ilallah is the only assignment of extreme **Barakah** (blessing) from Allah when His Angels protect and accompany a **Da'ee** when he is in the field of **Dawah Ilallah,** as described in **Verses # 30-32 of Surah Fussilat.**

إِنَّ الَّذِينَ قَالُوا رَبُّنَا اللَّهُ ثُمَّ اسْتَقَامُوا تَتَنَزَّلُ عَلَيْهِمُ الْمَلَائِكَةُ أَلَّا تَخَافُوا وَلَا تَحْزَنُوا وَأَبْشِرُوا بِالْجَنَّةِ الَّتِي كُنْتُمْ تُوعَدُونَ نَحْنُ أَوْلِيَاؤُكُمْ فِي الْحَيَاةِ الدُّنْيَا وَفِي الْآخِرَةِ وَلَكُمْ فِيهَا مَا تَشْتَهِي أَنْفُسُكُمْ وَلَكُمْ فِيهَا مَا تَدَّعُونَ نُزُلًا مِنْ غَفُورٍ رَحِيمٍ

"Lo! Those who say: Our Lord is Allah, and afterward are upright; the angels descend upon them, saying: Fear not nor grieve, but hear good tidings of the Paradise which ye are promised."
"We are your protecting friends in the life of the world and in the Heareafter. There ye will have (all) that your souls desire, and there ye will have (all) for which ye pray."
"A gift of welcome from the Forgiving, the Merciful."

[Qur'an, Surah Al-Fussilat, 41: 30-32]

A **Da'ee** gets the blessings of Allah in this world as well in Akhirah. There is no other surest way to get success (**Al-Falah**) here and in the Hereafter. There is no short-cut in Islam, and the Muslim **Ummah** must keep aloof from all such methods.

- "Unamta 'Alayhim":

This fixes the tone of our personal **'Ebadah**, its nature, its concept, its growth, its dynamism and all its comprehensiveness. The worshippers should follow its contents as a constant source of inspiration while reciting **Al-Fatiha**, especially during their nightly prayers. Insha Allah, they will have a special taste of it when beseeching from their Lord in all humbleness and sublimity on a **"person to person basis"** while crying and imploring and with tears rolling down their cheeks. Allah (SWT) sums up this state of His **'Abd** very eloquently in the following verses of **Al -Sajdah**:

إِنَّمَا يُؤْمِنُ بِآيَاتِنَا الَّذِينَ إِذَا ذُكِّرُوا بِهَا خَرُّوا سُجَّدًا وَسَبَّحُوا بِحَمْدِ رَبِّهِمْ وَهُمْ لَا يَسْتَكْبِرُونَ
تَتَجَافَىٰ جُنُوبُهُمْ عَنِ الْمَضَاجِعِ يَدْعُونَ رَبَّهُمْ خَوْفًا وَطَمَعًا وَمِمَّا رَزَقْنَاهُمْ يُنْفِقُونَ
فَلَا تَعْلَمُ نَفْسٌ مَا أُخْفِيَ لَهُمْ مِنْ قُرَّةِ أَعْيُنٍ جَزَاءً بِمَا كَانُوا يَعْمَلُونَ

"Only those believe in Our revelations who, when they are reminded of them, Fall down prostrate and hymn the praise of their Lord, and they are not scornful:

*Who forsake their beds to cry unto their Lord in fear and hope,
and spend of what we have bestowed on them.
No soul knows what is kept hid from them of joy, as a reward
for what they used to do."*

[Qur'an, Surah Al-Sajdah, 32: 15 -17]

Now let us examine the complexities of the second part of qualifying our prayer: **"Ehdina al- Sirat-al-Mustaqeem"** that we beg to Allah to show us and keep us on the path of righteousness **"but not the path of those who earn Your anger or of those who go astray"**:

B. THE ATTITUDE OF REJECTION:

"GHAYRIL MAGHDUBI 'ALAYHIM WA LAD-DALLEEN"

غَيْرِ الْمَغْضُوبِ عَلَيْهِمْ وَلَا الضَّالِّينَ

– [The path] Not of those who have been condemned [by You], nor of those who go astray.

In the context of Guidance from Allah, His **"Abd"** [slave] seems to be very particular in specifying his urge for guidance by qualifying his supplication by saying: **the path of those whom O Allah You rewarded handsomely but not the path of those who stand condemned by You or who have gone astray (and lost the guidance from their Lord).**

In the very first Section of **Surah Al-Baqarah**, at the very outset Allah (SWT) divided humanity, not on the basis of color, race, wealth, language or geographical boundaries, but on the criterion of **Iman** (faith), the believers in Him and the disbelievers and in between the two the hypocrites. Those who believe in Him and carve out their life as He ordains, struggle for establishing His authority on self, family and the society in which they live to attain His pleasure will be rewarded by Allah **[Unamta 'Alayhim] and be** placed in the category of **Al-Siddiqeen, Al-Shuhadah & Al-Saleheen** on the Day of Judgment – a mark of eternal bliss from their Lord.

Whereas those who disbelieve in Him, disobey his appointed messengers, discard His **Deen**, the system of life that He sent for their guidance, oppose its establishment tooth and nail with all means, carry a whirlwind propaganda campaign against it day in and day out, raise armed resistance to kill the Messenger and his beloved companions, **do fall under two well defined categories:**

1. <u>Al-Maghdub:</u>

The **"Condemned"** are those on whom Allah shows His **"Ghadab"** (wrath). It stands synonymous with the evil consequences which man brings upon himself by willfully rejecting Divine Guidance and acting contrary to His injunctions," [**<u>The Message of the Qur'an – Muhammad Asad</u>]**

The **"Maghdubeen"** - the Condemned are those to whom Allah's guidance came through His appointed messengers but they refused to accept it out of arrogance. They denied the Messenger of the time knowingly that he was His Messenger. They opposed him and the message tooth and nail. They killed many Prophets, conspired against them and distorted their teachings. They very often challenged them by ridiculing the message and the warnings of God's inevitable punishment here in this World and in the Hereafter, if they continued to make fun of warnings after warnings from God. They didn't pay any heed to the Guidance from their Lord or His constant warnings.

This has happened with almost all the Messengers of Allah without any exception. The reasons for this state of man's treatment – to accept or reject Allah's guidance and His Messenger - are engraved within human genes as ordained in **Verse # 7 to 10 of Surah # 91: Al-Shams:**

وَنَفْسٍ وَمَا سَوَّاهَا - فَأَلْهَمَهَا فُجُورَهَا وَتَقْوَاهَا
قَدْ أَفْلَحَ مَنْ زَكَّاهَا - وَقَدْ خَابَ مَنْ دَسَّاهَا

"Consider the human self, and how it is formed in accordance with what it is meant to be; and how it is imbued with moral failings as well as with consciousness of God.
He is indeed successful who causes this [self] to grow in purity and [truly] he is indeed a failure who buries it [in darkness–a matter of free choice."

[Qur'an, Surah Al-Shams, 91: 7 -10]

Thus, man carries both the properties and the characteristics to be good or to become bad and that would be through his or her free will. He also possesses the sense of recognizing good from bad. The cause of this far reaching choice also lies within human beings. **That is his test and accordingly he will be rewarded on the Day of Judgment if his choice was for "Right" on earth and will be punished if his choice was for "wrong." Had this free-choice not been given to man, the entire concept of accountability would have become meaningless, a farce.**

As stated earlier, man was created by Allah with three strong natural urges – urge for rest or sleep, hunger/thirst and the urge for sex when reaching maturity, with one freewill or free choice to meet these urges the way he/she likes. These urges are natural instincts and are essential for human growth, nourishment and the continuation of the human species on earth.

Allah created this universe and what it contains for man to explore and use for the satisfaction of his/her urges. It was the infinite knowledge of the Creator and Sustainer that man with his freewill would fill the earth with **Fasad** (transgression), **Zulm** (oppression) and bloodshed in acquiring and possessing the resources of his abode for the satisfaction of his urges, if he did not follow the 'right path" and learn how to live in moderation on earth. That is why He descended the first man, Adam on earth with clear Guidance and His "commitment" to continue sending the Guidance on how to act, live and behave on earth when it would become lost due to human innovations, mutilations and neglect.

Man could not maintain his commitment to Allah to follow His Guidance. His strong urges overpower him oft and on; whereas many follow His Guidance and live on earth as ordained by their Creator and Sustainer. Thus, many who disobey His directives get punished and stand **"condemned"** [with "Ghadab" – Allah's wrath]; whereas there are many who follow His Guidance and will be rewarded.

The entire pagan world through the ages has negated the guidance from the Creator and Sustainer and worshiped a lot of animate and inanimate objects. They made them equal to God, prostrated before them and deviated from the path of righteousness. The **Qur'an** draws a vivid picture of the inexcusable position of these people through **Verses # 1 to 6 of Surah # 6: Al-An'am** and in many other **Verses,** especially in Makkan **Surahs**. They all were **"condemned"** and were totally destroyed and annihilated from the surface of the earth for good in consequence of their denial of God and resorting to idol worshipping. The **Qur'an** gives a summary of

eight such nations with a brief historical perspective of each, with only one exception, and that is of the Jewish people or the "Sons of Israel" **[Bani Israel].** Theirs was and is a different story and hence it needed a separate discussion in detail as their history of rebellion against Allah is treacherous, multifarious and of defiance even to this day. Those who stand condemned and destroyed were **the people of Noah, 'Aad, Hud, Thamud, Lot, Sa'leh, Shu'ayb [Ref: Qur'an, Surah # 11 – HUD]** and many more nations who passed through the ages but their accounts are not given in the **Qur'an** and Allah referred them as **"Lam Naqsus"** – whose stories are untold. Human history is full of obscurity. It hardly covers a period of five thousand years. There are many "black holes" even in this period that presents only a scratchy account here and there limited to stories of some monarchs and their conquests. Human history, thus, does not present the complete account of all the people that ever lived on earth. Likewise, the Qur'an is also keeping silence about these dark periods that are obscured from human history.

THE ACCOUNT OF BANI ISRAEL:

The history of Bani Israel, unique amongst the nations, starts from the time of Prophet Ibrahim (AS) who was born in 2100 BC in UR, Iraq to an idolater father A'zar. He was among the progenies of prophet Noah (AS). Sir Leonard Woolley in his book "Abraham," published in London in 1935, narrates his life history that mostly corresponds with the truthful account given in the **Qur'an**, the only Book that elaborates the story of Abraham and his progenies. The story of Abraham is about 4200 years old. Abraham was **appointed as the leader of mankind** *[Inni Ja'iluka linnasi Imama]* when he came out successful from all the trials through which he passed as narrated in the Qur'an in **verse # 124 of Surah # 2: Al-Baqarah:**

وَإِذِ ابْتَلَىٰ إِبْرَاهِيمَ رَبُّهُ بِكَلِمَاتٍ فَأَتَمَّهُنَّ قَالَ إِنِّي جَاعِلُكَ لِلنَّاسِ
إِمَامًا قَالَ وَمِنْ ذُرِّيَّتِي قَالَ لَا يَنَالُ عَهْدِي الظَّالِمِينَ

"And (remember) when his Lord tried Abraham with (His) commands and he fulfilled them, He [Allah] said: Lo! I have appointed thee the leader of mankind. (Abraham} said: And of my offspring (will there be leaders)? He [Allah] said: My covenant includes not wrong-doers."

[Qur'an, Surah Al-Baqarah, 2: 124]

The cherished position of the leadership of mankind, though covetous, was full of responsibilities to guide the destiny of mankind in the light of Guidance that was constantly coming to them through a chain of Prophets for over two thousand years, form Jacob to Jesus (May Allah be pleased with all of them), each reminding the people of Israel to follow and fulfill their obligations to Allah and His **Deen**. Prophet Moses (AS), Prophet David and Prophet Solomon

(AS) established the mighty Kingdom of God on earth in terms of the Torah, the then Book of Guidance from Allah, but their progenies could not hold it intact. They lost it along with the guidance by making a lot of innovations in its original text. They were now following the Talmud which contains about 610 laws created by Rabbis and only two more that are from the Torah. The State of Bani Israel was totally ransacked twice: First by Babylonian King Bakhte Nasar in 587 BC, and the second time by the Romans in 70 AD in consequence of their misdeeds and creating **Fasad** (transgression) on earth. The **Qur'an** referred to these historical events in **Verse # 4 of Surah # 17 of Bani Israel.**

وَقَضَيْنَا إِلَىٰ بَنِي إِسْرَائِيلَ فِي الْكِتَابِ لَتُفْسِدُنَّ فِي الْأَرْضِ مَرَّتَيْنِ وَلَتَعْلُنَّ عُلُوًّا كَبِيرًا

"And We decreed for the children of Bani Israel in the Scripture: Ye verily will work corruption in the earth twice, and ye will become great tyrants."

[Qur'an, Surah Bani Israel, 17: 4]

Bani Israel, at that point of history, were the appointed leaders of mankind. Instead of calling humanity to the fold of its Creator and Sustainer they fell prey to worldly gains, luxuries and lusts, and were bogged down in fighting amongst themselves. They lost the heritage of King David and Solomon, along with the Guidance that was given to them to run human affairs as ordained by Allah. They personified their God as their own God, denied and disobeyed their Lord and His directives time and again and refused to follow the appointed Prophets of God, while killing some of them and totally denying many. They neither followed the guidance from Allah nor invited others to follow it. The History of Bani Israel is full of such deplorable events. **The Qur'an presents a panoramic view of their list of crimes from Verse # 40 to Verse # 121 in detail in Surah Al-Baqarah. They total twenty seven [27] in number. These crimes are very alarming and audacious in nature against the supreme authority of Allah. In consequence, they** were dethroned from the position of world leadership and allowed to live in the state of ignominy, disgrace and perpetual hate for about one thousand, nine hundred and fifty years as the "Al-Maghdubeen" (the most Condemned) in the annals of human history. The Qur'an depicts this picture very eloquently;

ضُرِبَتْ عَلَيْهِمُ الذِّلَّةُ أَيْنَ مَا ثُقِفُوا إِلَّا بِحَبْلٍ مِنَ اللَّهِ وَحَبْلٍ مِنَ النَّاسِ وَبَاءُوا بِغَضَبٍ مِنَ اللَّهِ وَضُرِبَتْ عَلَيْهِمُ الْمَسْكَنَةُ ۚ ذَٰلِكَ بِأَنَّهُمْ كَانُوا يَكْفُرُونَ بِآيَاتِ اللَّهِ وَيَقْتُلُونَ الْأَنْبِيَاءَ بِغَيْرِ حَقٍّ ۚ ذَٰلِكَ بِمَا عَصَوْا وَكَانُوا يَعْتَدُونَ

"Ignominy shall be their portion wheresoever they are found save (where they grasp) a rope from Allah and a rope from men [when they kept the Covenant "temporarily" for a couple of years which the Prophet (S) had made with the Jews and Arab Tribes at Madinah]. They have incurred anger from their Lord, and wretchedness is laid upon them. That is because they used to disbelieve the revelations of Allah, and slew the Prophets wrongfully. That is because they were rebellious and used to transgress."
[Qur'an, Surah Al-'Imran, 3: 112]

Only in the twentieth century, Jews as a people got "some respite" in 1948, not on their own accord, but with the help and support through the conspiracy hatched jointly by British, the USA, France and Russia, starting with the Balfour Declaration of 1917 and culminating with the combined resolution of five permanent members of the Security Council of UNO towards establishing the State of Israeli in Palestine on May 14, 1948. If today these "dominant" powers withdraw their intensive support, the **"artificial" State of Israel** placed in the heart of Muslim world will not be able to survive even for a few days. The verdict of the Qur'an as quoted above is absolutely clear and commanding for all times to come.

This completes the list of nations that stand condemned as "Al-Maghdub" through human history. All are dead and gone

with the wind, <u>except Bani Israel</u> who are left on earth alive under the overall planning of Allah as the living embodiment of those who violated His Guidance, disobeyed Him and His appointed Prophets of their time and were lost in their pursuit of satisfaction of their urges through exercising their own freewill.

The case of Bani Israel is a TEST case for the Muslim Ummah that was elevated on earth in their place as the <u>"Best of Nations,"</u> the <u>"Ummatun Wasatun"</u> and the <u>"Leaders of mankind"</u> to call humanity to the fold of Allah, eradicate the evils (Munkar), establish the <u>Ma'ruf</u>, deliver Justice (Al-Qist) to suffering humanity and stand in the "witness" box of history to fulfill the obligation of <u>"Shahadah Al-Annas"</u> as ordained by Allah (SWT) in <u>Verse # 143 of Al-Baqarah:</u>

وَكَذَٰلِكَ جَعَلْنَاكُمْ أُمَّةً وَسَطًا لِتَكُونُوا شُهَدَاءَ عَلَى النَّاسِ وَيَكُونَ
الرَّسُولُ عَلَيْكُمْ شَهِيدًا

"And, thus, We have willed (appointed) you to be a community of the middle way [a community that keeps an equitable balance between extremes and is realistic in its appreciation of man's nature] so that [with your lives] you might bear witness to the truth before all mankind and that the Apostle might bear witness to it before you."
[Qur'an, Surah Al-Baqarah. 2: 143]

The history of Al-Maghdubeen covering the living memories [that is, of Bani Israel's past and the present], is serving as a big lesson to the Muslim Ummah: That is, if they don't live up to their assignment, as it was given to the people of Israel, they are bound to face the same consequences as Jews have faced all through their history. In fact, Muslims are encountering the same fate of ignominy and disgrace as they are committing the same crime of neglecting their paramount assignment of Dawah Ilallah and struggle for the Iqamah of Allah's Deen. They are no exception to Allah's rule of <u>"crime</u>

and punishment." Allah has left the Jews as a living nation on earth for Muslims to have fear of Allah and take lessons both from their past and present, while always praying to their Lord; O Allah! Keep us away from the path of Al-Maghdubeen"

2. **WA LA AL-DALLEEN** – [And] nor [the path] of those who go astray:

وَلَا الضَّالِّينَ

Human beings have been treating the Guidance from their Creator and Sustainer in two ways: either denying and disobeying His authority altogether, rejecting the Messengers and the message totally or believing in Him and His authority but making partners with Allah (SWT) in His person and in His attributes, or making **"Ghuluw"** (exaggeration) in their religious beliefs and practices through innovations. The first behavior is that of **Al-Maghdubeen** (the condemned ones), and the second behavior is that of **Al-Dalleen** (the ones who go astray).

As regards the first category, I have shared their fate and condition in detail   above. Now the condition of those who fall in the category of **"Al-Dalleen"** should be discussed so that their characteristics become crystal clear, helping the Muslim **Ummah** in recognizing the people whose position with Allah is extremely precarious and hence **they must keep aloof from either of the two** categories, **while imploring to their Lord and Sustainer of this cosmos for Guidance to follow only the "Straight Path."**

Man by nature seeks some powerful or dominant authority to surrender to, show his allegiance to obey his commands, turn to it for help at time of distress and beg solace in heart and mind while surrendering to that source. This natural urge in human beings has always been exploited and instigated by "clever" people to their benefit, instigating people to worship the mighty kings or natural phenomenon and its manifestations: stones, rivers, trees, animals, down to human organs of procreation. The entire myth of idol-worshipping around the world, whether of Greek, Roman or Indian mythology, is surrounded with the reflection of the human weakness to surrender to power.

The pagan world is infested with such stories that are ceded with this inherent human psychology, forgetting the paramount concept that God created this universe and what it contains for man to be at His service as harnessed by Him for the benefit of man at the very outset of His creation. In consequence, man is suffering with extreme humiliation when bowing his head to these animate and inanimate objects or his own fellow beings in subordination, and degrading to the stage of **"Asfala Safileen" – the lowest of the low: [Qur'an, Surah Al-Teen, 95: 5].** *This is the genesis of the people who go astray.*

However, man's tragedy does not end here. In search of powerful phenomenon to surrender to, he responds to the call of the Messengers of God and accepts His supreme authority as Creator and Sustainer. But amongst those there are many who do not submit to Him in totality and start making partners with His person or attributes and commit the most sinful crime of **"Shirk" (Associating partners with Allah).**

Before the advent of Islam, Arabs were believing in Allah as the supreme authority but disputing how He alone could run the affairs of this vast cosmos. So they invented many idols as His partners/assistants and divided His Kingdom in various sectors, making one idol in charge of each, taking it as the surest way to reach God and get from Him anything that they wanted through their idol's intercession. Through this self-created deception idolatry came into existence everywhere in human society since the emergence of man on earth and it continues even to this day and "perhaps" till eternity. Thus, the concept of God as supreme authority is present in the background in almost all the religions or faiths throughout the pagan world, but it is infested with idolatry and **Shirk** which Allah abhors.

Allah (SWT) appointed His Messengers to correct the situation, so man could get rid of these fallacies of human thinking, and surrender to one and only one God who is their Sustainer. Many humans, primarily, accepted the Messengers and the authority of God, but with the passage of time the followers deviated: either making partners with His authority, as stated above, or exaggerating the provisions of Deen. They went on adding more and more rituals of **'Ebadah** that were not there originally and thus giving their faith a totally new shape. It could have been either through exaggerations, curtailments or making new interpretations of its injunctions, losing the originality of **Deen** altogether in its wake. A big chunk of humanity, perhaps more than half of the world's population, is drowned in **Shirk**, making partners with the most puritan Monotheistic authority of the Creator and Sustainer of this cosmos. What a horrible tragedy it is! Unfortunately, many Institutions on a global level are serving to promote these deviated paths. **The Inter-Faith Dialogues is one of them. Those who have already lost the Guidance are determined to see that others too should lose it or keep it in abeyance, and the Muslims are their outspoken targets**.

Prophet Jesus [pbuh] called the **people of Bani Israel** to the fold of their Creator and Sustainer, delivered the Guidance from their Lord in the form of the Book, "**Injeel**" (Gospel) and exhorted them to be obedient to God alone. The Jews refused him and were ultimately prepared to put him to gallows but Allah (SWT) raised him to heaven, which is categorically confirmed by the **Qur'an** in **Verse # 157 – 158 of Surah # 4 of Al-Nisa**

وَقَوْلِهِمْ إِنَّا قَتَلْنَا الْمَسِيحَ عِيسَى ابْنَ مَرْيَمَ رَسُولَ اللَّهِ وَمَا قَتَلُوهُ وَمَا صَلَبُوهُ وَلَكِنْ شُبِّهَ لَهُمْ وَإِنَّ الَّذِينَ اخْتَلَفُوا فِيهِ لَفِي شَكٍّ مِنْهُ مَا لَهُمْ بِهِ مِنْ عِلْمٍ إِلَّا اتِّبَاعَ الظَّنِّ وَمَا قَتَلُوهُ يَقِينًا بَلْ رَفَعَهُ اللَّهُ إِلَيْهِ وَكَانَ اللَّهُ عَزِيزًا حَكِيمًا

"And because of their saying: We slew the Messiah Jesus son of Mary, Allah's messenger – They slew him not nor crucified, but it appeared so unto them; and lo! those who disagree concerning it are in doubt thereof; they have no knowledge thereof save pursuit of a conjuncture; they slew him not for certain."

"But Allah took him up unto Himself, Allah was ever Mighty, Wise."

[Qur'an, Surah al-Nisa, 4: 157 -156]

Later on, the followers of Prophet Jesus [pbuh] who were "Muslims,"
obedient to God alone, adopted the name of "Christians" and their religion as Christianity, and they made a lot of exaggerations in their faith and mode of worship. Out of exaggerated love for Jesus, they made him the "Son of God" at the Council of Nicea in May 325 AD through a Royal decree and a year later, added "Divinity' to his mother Mary. **They deviated from the Straight Path that was shown to them by Prophet Jesus (pbuh).** Their march to such extremes continued unabated. **Many resorted to abstinence, renounced the world and its bounties, became hermits and saints, giving extreme hardship to their bodies, contrary to the original teachings of Jesus Christ and, thus, had gone astray, falling into the second category - the "Al-Dalleen."** They believed in God but made Jesus, the Prophet of God, 'His son,' and added the concept of Trinity to the pure ideology of Monotheism.

The Christians conveniently disposed of the paramount concept of accountability on the Day of Judgment and innovated the dogma of just "Belief in Jesus" as sufficient for "Salvation" in the life Hereafter. It is their own creation and there is no logic behind it. Thus, Christianity totally deviated and lost the Guidance that was brought by Prophet Jesus (pbuh) who was appointed as Messenger to Bani Israel. **What a great tragedy this was and is!** Jews refused to accept him as the Messenger of God, though they were waiting for the Messiah, and the Christians assigned Divinity to him. Thus, both lost the Straight Path, the Guidance from their Lord, and are wandering in the wilderness of their own self-created myths and dogmas and waiting now for the second coming of Jesus, or for their Messiah, when the fate of both dogmatic religions will be decided for good. The Prophecies of Muhammad (S) are very clear in this respect.

This explains why a conscious Muslim or Muslimah asks Allah (SWT): O Allah! Guide me, show me and keep me on "Sirat Al-Mustaqeem", (the Straight Path), qualifying <u>immediately</u> his/her statement by adding, "<u>The Path of those whom You have blessed and rewarded and not the path of those whom You have condemned and not of those who have gone astray.</u>"

And a Mu'min echoes his/her most comprehensive and the most cherished Du'a (supplication) that Al-Fateha brilliantly spells out by saying loudly or in his/her heart; Ameen!

CHAPTER – 5

SUMMATION OF AL-FATEHA AS "PREFACE TO THE QUR'AN": Al-Fateha can be summarized into four sections:

1, ASSERTION: Allah is **Al-Rahman** and **Al-Raheem**, and by virtue of these two inherent attributes He is **"Rabbul 'Alameen,"** the Sustainer of this cosmos. He is equally sustaining man with all that he needs on earth and maintaining this universe to enable man to live in peace and comfort with clear understanding and assertion that one day all humans will be accountable to Him for how they lived and behaved on earth (in obedience to Him or in the state of denial and disobedience), when His authority will be supreme and absolute on that Day of Judgment. It confirms the **inevitability of Akhirah** beyond any shadow of doubt and man must live by that.

2. CONFESSION: This assertion brings man to the doorsteps of the Sovereign of this universe in all humility, confessing: **"IYYAKA NA'BUDU"** [We worship Thee alone in every walk of life] and begging **"IYYAKA NASTA'EEN"** [We seek help only from Thee for all our needs and urges].

- This perfects the total authority of Allah, confessing and **demonstrating the total semblance of Monotheism (Tawheed),** the topmost reality/truth of this cosmos, the **essence of Iman Billah.**

- This cuts man off from dependence of all worldly sources for help and puts him at the doorstep of his Lord to beg each and every thing from Him, removing even the slightest atom of **Shirk** form his life altogether. His **Iman** becomes as pure as 24 carat gold.

- This completes the total surrender of man to the authority of his Creator and Sustainer, declaring that he has no choice but to surrender to Him for all of his needs and urgencies, the culminating point and the zenith of his **"Tawakkal" at-Allah** [total dependence on Allah, **the climax of Iman Billah].**

3. IMPLORING FOR GUIDANCE - THE GRESATEST NEED OF MAN:

Man could not and cannot deliver the Guidance to his own species as he is totally incompetent in this respect, and whatever he did through the ages in this account it failed bitterly, filling human society only with confusion, chaos, disorder and bloodshed. This urgent and topmost need of man brings him begging to the Lord of this Cosmos to favor him with His Divine Guidance that He arranges for mankind as per His "commitment" through His appointed Messengers who delivered and demonstrated to the world how to act, live and behave on earth by presenting their respective life patterns as a model to be followed by His followers.

[This entire topic I have, Alhamdulillah, discussed separately in my book: **The Greatest Need of Man."** *It is available on my Website:* WWW.dawahinamericas.com. *For understanding all the complexities of the situation, readers should go through it. It establishes why our Greatest Need is Guidance and nothing else, and it can be delivered only by our Creator and Sustainer and none else.]*

- This brings us to the third point of the **"Preface to the Qur'an"** – the **Risalah -** (Prophethood). The first two points of the Preface – **Tawheed (Monotheism) and Akhirah (The Hereafter),** have been covered as summarized above. **Al-Fateha** is the Preface to the **Qur'an** and the three paramount themes of the **Qur'an –Tawheed, Akhirah and Risalah,** have been institutionalized in sequence in the most effective and briefest possible way, keeping **all its impact and significance at the highest order** in such a way that man understands the glimpses of the entire teachings of the **Qur'an** in the seven capsule **verses** of **Al-Fateha.** Man can memorize it easily and recite it many a times in a day in his **Salah,** and can become its model in his practical life if he follows its contents both in letter and spirit as his life long pursuit.

Man's urge for Guidance is his Greatest Need which he could get only from Allah's appointed Messengers. The **Qur'an** covers the spectrum of the chain of Messengers of Allah that were raised for the guidance of mankind in a continuous process from Adam to Mohammad [May Allah bless all of them]. The **Qur'an** gives the account of all the prominent Messengers/Prophets of Allah and **Al-Fateha** surmounts it beautifully by presenting Guidance as man's greatest need and urgency, begging for the Straight Path of those whom Allah rewarded immensely and not of those who stand condemned and have gone astray.

- **Allah Rabbul 'Alameen** has been arranging Guidance for man as and when needed. The question arises as to how man behaved or is behaving with the guidance from his Master? **How he treated it in the past or is treating it now in the context of the modern world?** This brings us to the concluding part of **Al-Fateha** that exposes the behavior of man, how he dealt with or is dealing with this Guidance - obediently as the servant of Allah or disobediently in revolt to His authority.

4. **TREATMENT OF GUIDANCE:** It is a very delicate situation. Man is enjoying all the facilities and bounties on earth that his Creator and Sustainer has provided and harnessed for him to enjoy as per his freewill or the way he likes; but he behaves very differently with the Guidance that Allah has formally arranged for him through His appointed Messengers to enable him to live on earth in peace and in harmony with his species. By exercising his free will, man could get the best of both worlds by following it meticulously or rejecting it out of arrogance or ignorance and become the loser everywhere. This behavior of man has persisted throughout human history from its very outset and continues to be so even to this day and perhaps for ages to come till eternity. This is the intimate game of his free will. When man becomes the master of his physical urges he tries to live in moderation and follows the Guidance from his Lord; but whenever he is overpowered or carried away by his natural instincts and urges, he has ignored His guidance and filled his abode with **Fasad**, disorder and bloodshed. In consequence, either

he stands in the category whom his Lord rewards or in the group of those whom He condemns, depending on the attitude of man toward the Guidance from his Creator and Sustainer...

The **Qur'an** gives accounts of both categories of people, sometimes in brief and sometimes in detail, in the historical perspective of each, elaborating on their respective treatment and behavior toward Allah's Guidance and the nature of their crimes, how they treated His Messengers and the message - * leading a life of total obedience to Allah alone, * feeling always accountable to Him for all actions and deeds on earth and, * keeping the life-pattern of the Messenger of the time as a model to follow in every walk of life. This is the beauty of the **Qur'an** that it has put this entire scenario of human's behavior of **"acceptance or rejection of the Guidance and its net result"** in two most precise and concise phrases: **Sirat-alladhina Unamta 'Alayhim"** and **"Ghayril-Maghdubi 'Alayhim Waladdalleen" - The path of those whom You rewarded; not the path of those whom You have condemned or (of those) who go astray.**

Thus, **Al-Fateha** miraculously presents the **Preface of "the Qur'an in miniature,"** the essence of its message, the **Greatest Need of man and human behavior along with it in seven brief and well-articulated sentences that a Muslim repeats many times a day, every day, feeling always its depth and empowering effect anew, never feel tiring of its repetition, cherishing always a new pleasure and contentment in heart and mind that he has presented the constant echoing sound of his inner self to the Supreme authority of this cosmos who is his Lord, the Sustainer, and with complete confidence that his Lord is listening and responding to his heartfelt humble supplications wherever he is and whatever he is doing. He is the closest to me with no middle-man in between us and He is my best Protector. Let us see how our Creator and Sustainer responds to my paramount prayers and submissions that Al-Fateha   contains   with   the   depth   of   an   ocean.**

CHAPTER – 6

EVALUATION OF AL-FATEHA FROM THE POINT OF SUBMISSION & SUPPLICATION – DU'A

The format of **Al-Fateha** is "**Du'ayeeyah**" (**Supplication**). It is the urge of one's inner self that feeling the insurmountable favors and bounties of Allah in his person and scattered all around this universe for his sustenance and maintenance on this earth, he expresses his paramount gratitude -"**Shukr**" to **Rabbul-al-'Alameen**, the Lord of this cosmos. This state of heart and mind brings him to surrender to his Master entirely, presenting his Greatest Need of life at His doorstep while imploring Him for the "**Sirat Al-Mustaqeem**" (the Straight path), the path of those whom He rewarded and not the path of those whom He **"condemned"** or **who go astray**. This entire scenario of total surrender and submission to Allah (SWT), imploring Him for Guidance on how to live, act and behave while living on this earth is enveloped just into seven small but very comprehensive **Verses** (**Ayah**), bringing immediate response from the Creator and Sustainer, with a unique format of **acceptance** of each segment of the prayer that **Al-Fateha** contains.

Muslims recite **Al-Fateha** many a times in a day as an obligatory part of their five times daily prayers, as no **Salah** will be acceptable to Allah if it is not recited therein: "**La Salata leman lam Yaqrau bil-Fatihatul-Kitab.** It is from a Hadith narrated by both Bukhari and Muslim. The person who forgets to recite **Al- Fateha** in **Salah**, his **Salah** is lost.

This establishes the **significance of Al-Fateha** in our day to day life. As discussed earlier, Muslims recite it at least seventeen times a day in Obligatory prayers, feeling the continuous response from Allah (SWT) in the form of acceptance or the grant of their humble prayers. **It opens a unique chapter of man's direct relation with his Creator and Sustainer with a clear assurance that our prayers are accepted right at the moment we beseech,** provided we recite them clearly, understand its contents with total devotion and complete presence of mind, heart and soul. We should keep totally in view: to whom we are begging; for what we are begging; what commitment we are making every time; and realizing fully well how are we behaving with the Guidance that He, in His infinite mercy, has sent to us through His appointed Messenger Muhammad Rasulullah (S).

If a Muslim fulfills these conditions, he attains his personal accession (Mi'raj) to Allah each time when he/she stands in **Salah** as **Salah** is the **"Mi'raj-ul- Mu'mineen"** [a means of accession of the **Mu'min** to Allah (SWT)]. If a Muslim attains this accession each time he/she stands for **Salah**, what better success in life could an individual think to accomplish while he/she is still in his/her mortal frame. No success would be better than this that **he is directly involved in a live dialogue with Allah (SWT),** the Lord of this cosmos. The beauty of this **humble submission** knows no bounds when a Muslim gets up late in the night, **offers Salat-ut-Tahajjud** when the world is sleeping and **he enters in secret communication with his Master** under the constant shadow of "**fear and hope**" [Ref: Qur'an, Al-A'raf. 7: 55-56 & 205] that his Sustainer is listening to his humble submission and accepting all that he is putting before Him. The coveted blessings of our Lord are limitless.

ادْعُوا رَبَّكُمْ تَضَرُّعًا وَخُفْيَةً ۚ إِنَّهُ لَا يُحِبُّ الْمُعْتَدِينَ
وَلَا تُفْسِدُوا فِي الْأَرْضِ بَعْدَ إِصْلَاحِهَا وَادْعُوهُ خَوْفًا وَطَمَعًا ۚ إِنَّ
رَحْمَتَ اللَّهِ قَرِيبٌ مِنَ الْمُحْسِنِينَ

"(O mankind!) Call upon your Lord humbly and in secret. Lo! He loves not aggressors."
"Work not confusion in the earth after the fair ordering (thereof), and call on Him in fear and hope. Lo! the mercy of Allah is nigh unto the good."
[Qur'an, Surah Al-A'raf, 7: 55 56]

وَاذْكُرْ رَبَّكَ فِي نَفْسِكَ تَضَرُّعًا وَخِيفَةً وَدُونَ الْجَهْرِ مِنَ الْقَوْلِ
بِالْغُدُوّ وَالْآصَالِ
وَلَا تَكُنْ مِنَ الْغَافِلِينَ

"And do thou (O Muhammad) remember thy Lord within thyself <u>humbly and with awe</u>, below thy breath, at morn and evening. And be thou not of the neglectful."
<u>**[Qur'an, Surah Al-A'raf, 7: 205]**</u>

In fact, the bounties of this cosmos and His blessings all are for such brothers and sisters who live by the <u>Assertion</u>: "Iyyaka Na'budu wa Iyyaka Nasta'een." This is the Key to the success of a Mu'min in both the worlds. Once Muslims learn how to use this key to attain the <u>Falah</u>, this world will be theirs. <u>My humble efforts through this presentation may pave the way for all of us to raise our heads in the community of nations again as the savior of mankind and help humanity to get rid of the tyrants of our age.</u>

This <u>Hadith Qudsi</u> which is the corner stone of this prayer was narrated by Abu Hurairah (RA) and quoted by "Sahih Muslim," showing that when an "Abdullah" (slave of Allah] recites Al-Fateha with total devotions and submissions, its every word is acknowledged and accepted by Allah and His "ABD" (slave] gets what he/she begs from Him:

<u>THAT HADITH QUDSI IS QUOTED BELOW</u>

<u>"Abu Hurairah (RA) narrates from Rasulullah (S) that Allah (SWT) ordains:</u>

عَنْ أَبِي هُرَيْرَةَ ، عَنِ النَّبِيِّ ﷺ قَالَ : فَإِنِّي سَمِعْتُ رَسُولَ اللهِ ﷺ يَقُولُ : ﴿ قَالَ اللهُ تَعَالَى : قَسَمْتُ الصَّلَاةَ بَيْنِى وَبَيْنَ عَبْدِى نِصْفَيْنِ . وَلِعَبْدِي مَا سَأَلَ . فَإِذَا قَالَ الْعَبْدُ : الْحَمْدُ للهِ رَبِّ الْعَالَمِينَ . قَالَ اللهُ تَعَالَى: حَمِدَنِي عَبْدِي . وَإِذَا قَالَ : الرَّحْمَنِ الرَّحِيم . قَالَ اللهُ تَعَالَى : أَثْنَى عَلَيَّ عَبْدِي . وَإِذَا قَالَ : مَالِكِ يَوْمِ الدِّينِ . قَالَ : مَجَّدَنِي عَبْدِي ﴿وَقَالَ مَرَّةً : فَوَّضَ إِلَيَّ عَبْدِي﴾ فَإِذَا قَالَ : إِيَّاكَ نَعْبُدُ وَإِيَّاكَ نَسْتَعِينُ . قَالَ : هَذَا بَيْنِى وَبَيْنَ عَبْدِى وَلِعَبْدِي مَاسَأَلَ . فَإِذَا قَالَ : اهْدِنَا الصِّرَاطَ الْمُسْتَقِيمَ صِرَاطَ الَّذِينَ أَنْعَمْتَ عَلَيْهِمْ غَيْرِ الْمَغْضُوبِ عَلَيْهِمْ وَلَا الضَّالِّينَ . قَالَ: هَذَا لِعَبْدِي وَلِعَبْدِي مَا سَأَلَ ﴾ .

* "I have divided the **Salah** between Me and My **Abd** (slave) half and half – half is for Me and the other half is for My slave and **he will get what he asks for:**

* When My Abd recites '**Al-Hamdu Lillahey Rabbil 'Alameen,**' [immediately) Allah acknowledges that '**My slave has praised Me;**'

* And when he says, '**Al-Rahman Al-Raheem,**' Allah (SWT) responds (immediately) saying: '**My slave exalted Me;**

* And when he says: '**Ma'likey Yawmiddeen,**' (immediately) Allah's response comes: '**My slave glorified Me;**'

* And when he says, '**Iyyaka Na'budu Wa Iyyaka Nasta'een,**' He responds (forthwith) '**This is between Me and My slave and for My slave is what he asks for;**'

* And when he recites, '**Ehdina-al-Sirat-al-Mustaqeem' Sirat-alladhina Unamta 'Alayhim, Ghayril-Maghdubey 'Alayhim walad-dalleen,**' (the response immediately comes form Allah) '**This is for My slave and My slave will have all what he asks for'.**"

See what a realistic analytical response comes from Allah, fortifying the very depth of al-Fateha and what it envisages. How quickly the response comes from our Lord. It is meaningful. The moment the prayer comes out from the core of the heart of the Muslim, Allah (SWT) responds to it affirmatively with a categorical assurance that each urge of his inner self is granted forthwith. Can there be any better assurance towards the acceptance of our most solemn prayers than the quick and positive responses that continue to pour on us from our Lord, decorating our prayers with sure success? The appreciation of the beauty of these prayers, the gracefulness of the continuous response coming incessantly from the Supreme Lord of this cosmos and the quantum of His Mercy and magnanimity that He showers on His slave ('Abd) can be understood better if the comprehensiveness and the salient features of the meaningful supplication and its acceptance by Allah (SWT) are elaborated on further.

i. A Muslim, while standing and beginning his **Salah** must start it with the realization and conviction that he is going to be constantly involved in a two-way communication with the Lord of this universe **(Rabbul 'Alameen)** with the recitation of **Al-Fateha**. How fortunate he is and how Kind, Merciful and Compassionate his Lord is! **It would set the tone of his Salah at the very outset if he is mindful of this situation and he must continue this state to the end as he/she repeats Al-Fateha in every Rak'ah.**

ii. **Al-Fateha** must, therefore, always be recited keeping in mind that Allah (SWT) is responding to every word of it. Muslims must try to visualize the would-be forthcoming responses from their Lord, try to relish their fortune and resolve to transform their life in that frame as their ultimate destiny. **They must recite Al-Fateha slowly, consciously and giving a little momentary pause after each segment to relish the response from their Lord. Only then will they get the real taste of Salah.**

iii. The Du'a (prayer) must come from the depth of our heart with total presence of mind, understanding each word of it, expressing with rapt adoration, total devotion and complete realization what we are reciting and overwhelmed with extreme consciousness of the response that Allah (SWT) is according to His slaves instantaneously. **How fortunate we Muslims are!**

iv. This whole process helps in cementing the personal relation of an '**Abd** (slave) with his Master, assuring Him of his total commitment and, in response, getting His constant attention to His prayers and supplications, irrespective of time, place and situation...

v. At this stage, the slave of Allah (**'Abd**) feels that He is **"My GOD"** and I am "to live and die" for Him alone on this earth. This conscious resolution fills his heart with **"Yaqeen-ul-kamil"** (**complete conviction**) of total dependence on Allah - **"Tawakkal Al-Allah,"** the formidable position towards the attainment or the perfection of **"Iman Billah"** and what it demands from a **Mu'min**.

vi. This state of Iman empowers the Muslims not to extend the "beggars bowl" to anyone on earth except to their Lord.-rendering them to be the truthful models of **"Iyyaka Na'budu wa Iyyaka Nasta'een,"** This produces the real taste of **Iman** in a **Mu'min**, the fruits of his total Contentment.

vii. In **this requisite state of Iman, the Muslim becomes the symbol of "Shukr"** when Allah (SWT) favors him with His pleasure and bounties, and a symbol of **"Sabr"** (patience) when his Lord puts him to some test or trial that is inevitable for a **Mu'min** to test his **Iman**, polish the qualities of his heart and mind and give new impetus to the **Mu'min**. In both situations he learns to live the way his Sustainer ordains for him to live. In every situation, he will look towards Him with satisfaction, bearing an extreme sense of self-contentment, irrespective of where he is, what he is doing and how difficult the situation is. **It would gradually make a Muslim the symbol of "Sabr and Shukr," the most desirable and cherished characteristic of a Mu'min thereby transforming him into the trustworthy character of Da'ee Ilallah.**

viii. **This perpetual state of mind**, exercising, day and night, **with complete sense of surrender to Allah and with a total sense of realization that:**

*He is always with His slaves ('Abd) – ["Wa Huwa Ma'akum

Aynama Kuntum" – "He is with you wherever you are" - <u>Ref</u>
<u>Verse # 4 of Surah # 57, Al-Hadeed]</u>;

وَهُوَ مَعَكُمْ أَيْنَ مَا كُنْتُمْ

* Listening and responding immediately to all one's prayers as
and when his slave calls and entreats as Allah ordains in
Verse 186 of Surah Al- Baqarah:

وَإِذَا سَأَلَكَ عِبَادِي عَنِّي فَإِنِّي قَرِيبٌ أُجِيبُ دَعْوَةَ الدَّاعِ إِذَا دَعَانِ
فَلْيَسْتَجِيبُوا لِي وَلْيُؤْمِنُوا بِي لَعَلَّهُمْ يَرْشُدُونَ

*"And when My servants question thee concerning Me, then
surely I am nigh. I answer the prayer of the supplicant when he
cries unto Me. So let them hear My call and let them trust in
Me, in order that they may be led aright."*
[Qur'an, Surah Al-Baqarah, 2: 186]

* <u>Reminding</u> that we are His Vicegerent (<u>Khalifah</u>] on earth
and have to live here as per His directives. <u>[Ref: Surah Al-
Baqarah, Verses 30 - 38]</u>;
* <u>Only to glorify our Lord</u>, [Arise and warn and glorify Thy
Lord] - "Qum fa Andhir wa Rabbaka Fa-kabbir."   <u>[Qur'an,
Surah Al-Muddaththir, 54:2-3]</u>;

قُمْ فَأَنْذِرْ – وَرَبَّكَ فَكَبِّرْ

* <u>Establish His authority</u> on self, families, the societies in which
we live and the world at large as Allah ordains in <u>Verse 208of Al-
Baqarah: "Udkhulu fi Al-Silmi Kaffatan;"</u>

* <u>Struggle incessantly</u> for the <u>Iqamah of His Deen</u> with all that He
endowed us with – time, talent, energies and resources:

"…An Aqiymuddiyna wa la-tatafarraqu fiyh." "Establish the
Deen [of Allah] and be not divided therein…"   <u>[Qur'an, Surah
Al-Shurah, 42: 13]</u>;

أَنْ أَقِيمُوا الدِّينَ وَلَا تَتَفَرَّقُوا فِيهِ

* Enabling us to attain the truthful position of Da'ee Ilallah who is always accompanied by His angels while on earth and after death, "murmuring" in his ears about the glad tidings that Allah promises in Verses 30 - 32 of Surah 41 - Al-Fussilat, as quoted earlier. Angels always keep the company of a Da'ee Ilallah while on earth. What a grand success!

ix. This constant "Reminder" prepares the Muslim and Muslimah to undertake the only mission of his/her life that Allah ordains in Verses # 110 and 104 of Al-'Imran: "You are the best of the nations that has been raised up for mankind towards:

كُنْتُمْ خَيْرَ أُمَّةٍ أُخْرِجَتْ لِلنَّاسِ تَأْمُرُونَ بِالْمَعْرُوفِ وَتَنْهَوْنَ عَنِ الْمُنْكَرِ وَتُؤْمِنُونَ بِاللَّهِ

"You are the best community that has been raised up for mankind. You enjoin best conduct and forbid decency; and you believe in Allah…"
[Qur'an, Surah Al-'Imran, 3: 110]

وَلْتَكُنْ مِنْكُمْ أُمَّةٌ يَدْعُونَ إِلَى الْخَيْرِ وَيَأْمُرُونَ بِالْمَعْرُوفِ وَيَنْهَوْنَ عَنِ الْمُنْكَرِ ۚ وَأُولَٰئِكَ هُمُ الْمُفْلِحُونَ

"And let there be from you a people who invite to Khayr (goodness), and enjoin Ma'ruf (right conduct) and forbid Munkar (indecency)…"
[QUR'AN, Surah Al-'Imran, 3: 104]

_* Calling the people of the land to the fold of their Creator and Sustainer in a determined, an organized fashion, and in a continuous process till the contactees accept the Deen of Allah or prefer to remain in darkness of ignorance – the basic ingredients of Dawah Ilallah] - demonstrating the determination that Rasulullah (S) expressed to his uncle Abu Talib:

"If the idolaters put the sun in my right hand, the moon in my left, I will not give up the mission [of Dawah Ilallah] till either I succeed or give up my life in that pursuit." ["Seerah" Ibn Hisham]

* **Enjoining the right conduct,** putting collective efforts to establish the **"Ma'ruf"** [what is permissible and acceptable to all] in the society where the Muslim lives;

* **Forbidding indecency,** making every effort jointly and concertedly to eradicate the prevailing evils – **Al-Munkar** [what are not permissible or are prohibited] from the society;

* **These Dawah efforts are tantamount to fulfilling the obligation of Iqamatuddeen [establishing the Deen of Allah],** preparing every individual Muslim and Muslimah to contribute in every possible way towards accomplishing the mission of his/her life, enabling each of us to say to Allah (SWT) on the Day of Judgment when His authority will be Supreme **[Ma'likey Yawmiddeen]**, **"O Allah! What you gave us - life, time, talents and resources, all we put in Your way towards the establishment of Your Deen."** Only then may Allah accept our meaningful excuses, if any, that we make every effort in that direction, O Allah! But the success was not in our hands. Otherwise, our *neglect* of this prime-most obligation of our life towards Iqamah of His Deen and our frequent involvement in the luxuries of the worldly life will become the most disastrous things and all our **"lame-duck excuses"** will have no value for Allah (SWT) Who knows our heart and mind and what is hidden therein [Surah Al-Hadeed 57: 6]

وَهُوَ عَلِيمٌ بِذَاتِ الصُّدُورِ

* We have no choice but to perform our Salah carefully and act upon the echoing sounds of our heart and soul while reciting Al-Fateha, entreating and promising to Allah (SWT) to be His most obedient servants ['Ibad] living and dying only for Him till the last breath of our life.

x. This brings the "'Abd of Allah" to realize his ultimate position and responsibility on earth that through the process of **Dawah Ilallah**, he is to deliver the **"Al-Qist"** - **Justice**, to the suffering humanity, the ultimate objective for which all the Messengers of Allah were appointed on this earth as ordained in **Verse # 25 of Al-Hadeed:** and for the attainment of which **all the Prophets of Allah, Al-Siddiqeen, Al-Saleheen and Al-Shuhadah struggled hard FOR THE WHOLE OF THEIR LIFE for His Deen and whom He rewarded [Unamta 'Alayhim] immensely and made them our models till eternity.**

لَقَدْ أَرْسَلْنَا رُسُلَنَا بِالْبَيِّنَاتِ وَأَنْزَلْنَا مَعَهُمُ الْكِتَابَ وَالْمِيزَانَ لِيَقُومَ النَّاسُ بِالْقِسْطِ ۖ وَأَنْزَلْنَا الْحَدِيدَ فِيهِ بَأْسٌ شَدِيدٌ وَمَنَافِعُ لِلنَّاسِ وَلِيَعْلَمَ اللَّهُ مَنْ يَنْصُرُهُ وَرُسُلَهُ بِالْغَيْبِ ۚ إِنَّ اللَّهَ قَوِيٌّ عَزِيزٌ

"We verily sent forth Our Messengers [in a chain and in a continuous process] with all evidence with them, the Scripture and the Balance that mankind may observe [and establish] Al-Qist - Justice [right measures on earth] and He bestowed iron wherein is mighty power and (many) uses for mankind that Allah may know him who helps [stand up for] Him and His Messengers though unseen. Lo! Allah is Strong and Almighty"
[Qur'an, Surah Al-Hadeed, 57: 25]

There is no justice anywhere in the world today. All human rights are being denied to the oppressed. The poor, the needy and the have-nots are suffering the most. No UN and no International Court of Justice are of any use at this juncture. False and concocted wars are waged against the poor and downtrodden nations. The G 8 countries are imposing their economic and political will on the under-developed and the developing countries now in the form of WTO and Globalization of trade and commerce with no trade barriers. Humanity is crying as it was lamenting by the end of the sixth century AD when it had lost all the Divine Guidance from its Creator and Sustainer and was in waiting for more than 500 years for its savior who, by the grace of Allah, ultimately was born in 570 AD in Makkah. He (S) delivered the Divine System of Justice and peace to the world and established a Model Community/Ummah on that pattern within 23 years of his (S) life as the Messenger of Allah. With the help of the Divine Guidance, the Qur'an and Deen-Al-Haq, he (S) filled the earth with Justice in every walk of life.

The world has again come onto the same stage and is crying out for Justice and Peace but, unfortunately, the people who could repeat the illustrious history of their Prophet Muhammad (S) are sitting with hands crossed, though each member of the Muslim Ummah is committing to his/her Lord of this cosmos many a times throughout the day and night that <u>he/she is only obedient to Him and seeks help only from Him,</u> begs Hidayah only from Him on the lines He rewarded to His "slaves" who struggled for His Deen. Muslims have to come out of this anomalous situation, praying and begging to their Lord for something but doing some- thing else.   As a result, their condition is the same as that of the Jews and the Christians at the threshold of sixth century AD or of their own when Genghis Khan ransacked the Muslim world in the mid 12th. Century of the Christian era.

<u>Seeing the deplorable condition of the Muslim Ummah which is leading a life contrary to the spirit of Al-Fateha, Muslims now have no choice</u>. <u>They have to come out of their dilemma which is their own creation, by</u> truly following their Commitment to their Lord and follow the out-come of their humble prayers that they are making to the Creator and Sustainer of this Universe while reciting Al-Fateha and the generous "Commitment" that their Lord is making incessantly day and night in response. The onerous task of <u>reminding the Ummah to stand by this "double-track" commitment and thereby reaping its harvest</u> lies on the shoulders of the Muslim leadership around the world. They are already standing in the witness box of humanity and Allah (SWT) will ask each of them on the Day of Judgment: How they [the leaders, the Imams and

the Muslim scholars] fulfilled this responsibility and how the Muslim masses responded to it?

xi. The Zenith of a Mu'min: When a Muslim goes through this entire process – totally surrendering to the Lord of the universe consciously, obeying Him in every walk of life devotedly, sacrificing all that he/she possesses for establishing His authority on self, family and the society in which he/she lives solemnly, he/she may attain the coveted designations of **Al-Siddiqeen, Al-Saleheen and Al-Shuhadah** from his/her Lord.. Allah (SWT), in His infinite mercy, recognizes him/her, then, as His **"'Abd"** (slave), **the zenith of a Mu'min, and addresses him/her: O the Contented Soul** [Al-Nafsul-Mutmainnah] It would enable him/her to experience the most cherished scenario when meeting Allah (SWT) on the Day of Judgment: **When our Lord will address the contented soul as:**

$$يَا أَيَّتُهَا النَّفْسُ الْمُطْمَئِنَّةُ - ارْجِعِي إِلَى' رَبِّكِ رَاضِيَةً مَرْضِيَّةً$$
$$فَادْخُلِي فِي عِبَادِي - وَادْخُلِي جَنَّتِي$$

"O Contented Soul!
Return unto your Lord; content in His good pleasure!
Enter you among My bondmen!
Enter you My Garden."
[Qur'an, Surah Al-Fajr, 89: 27 -30]

THE HOPE: This all is possible to attain if the Muslims around the world understand <u>Al-Fateha</u>, the way Allah (SWT) ordains when they recite and try their utmost to live by its contents and spirit and fulfill the ideals that are put in its depth miraculously by our Sustainer. I have tried to elaborate the few brief sentences of Al-Fateha in my humble way, with the Hope that the Muslim Ummah may change its direction and fortune, if it learns through this process to respond correctly and courageously with what this <u>Preface of Al-Qur'an</u> demands from each of us to accomplish.

O Allah! Fulfill this cherished Hope of Your most humble servant ['Abd] who submits to You this most fervent prayer every day and night for years together, knowing fully well that You are listening but responding to it most appropriately in Your Majestic way categorically in the form of Your tragic "Complaint" to the Muslim Ummah which, unfortunately, is passing its "days and nights" in deep slumber and showing mostly only lip sympathy to Islam:

"HUM TU MA'EL BA KARAM HAIN KOI SA'EL HI NAHIN.
RAH DEKHLAYEN KISEY KOI RAHRAWAY MANZIL HI NAHIN"

> Translation: I am totally inclined to help, but there is no beggar [Applicant] to whom I can show the Path; there is no traveler marching towards the "Destiny."

This couplet of the Poet Iqbal [from "Answer to Shikwah"] exactly presents the existing state of the Muslim Ummah. Let us all commit to ourselves to change our fate and beg to Allah Rabbul 'Alameen – the Sustainer of this cosmos Who responds to our prayers instantaneously, and that is what Al-Fateha, the Preface to the Qur'an, demands. At least, let us correct our Salah and through that process correct our relations with the Lord of this Universe and, IN RETURN, get the Ummah out of its dilemma.

O Allah! Change the fate of the Muslim Ummah, fulfill our Hopes and save us from the self-created ignominy! AMEEN!

Shamim Siddiqi
6 Plant Lane, Westbury, NY
July 3, 2008, [End of my 80th year]
Website: WWW.dawahinamericas.com ;
E-mail: tsidd96472@aol.com

[Alhamdulillah, revisions completed: Friday July 18, 2008; August 2, 08 & 9/16/08. Edited Copy ready: November 24, 2008/November 30, 08/December 25, 08.

G L O S S A R Y

1. ABD:

Slave. All the humans are Allah's "Abd" [slaves]. They are to live on this earth for a while as His vicegerent but under His directives and commands that He manages to send for man through His appointed Messengers as and when His Guidance is lost due to human's innovations or interpolations. Man is to live on earth under His total obedience by exercising his/her freewill. Only then he/she will be recognized by Allah as His Abd and be rewarded accordingly.

2. AJR:

Reward. Man is living on earth as a responsible human being, feeling always accountable to Him for all his/her actions and deeds. The reward (AJR) of these deeds may be good, if he/she has been obedient to Him or may be bad if he was disobedient to Him and leading the life of an arrogant on earth.

3. Akhirah:

The Day of Resurrection/Judgment when every human being will face his/her Lord and will be accountable to Him for all his/her actions and deeds on earth — will be rewarded with eternal bliss of paradise if he/she has obeyed Him all through or will be thrown in the eternal ditch of fire if disobeyed Him throughout.

4. Allah:

It is the Arabic name of God. "Allah" is the proper name of the Creator and Sustainer of this cosmos and what it contains. It has always been used by Arabs for the Monotheistic authority of God. Allah is One and is only One. It is always masculine and Has no feminine gender. It is always in singular as Allah is One And it has no plural. The Arabic Bible also uses the word "Allah" not God at all.

5. Dawah Ilallah [DI]:

Calling the people to the fold of Allah – the Creator and Sustainer of this cosmos. DI is a determined, an organized and a continuous effort till the time either the addressees accept the authority of Allah, enter into His Deen Al-Islam and live like a Muslim [obedient to God alone] or decide otherwise. DI ends when it would envelop the entire humanity in its fold and the Da'ee is to carry out his/her effort till the last breath of life.

6. Deen Al- Islam:

Islam is a Deen – a system of life and not a religion as Judaism and Christianity are or have become. Islam covers and governs the entire spectrum of human life from birth to death and from cradle to grave both at individual and collective levels. Equally, Islam is a Movement at the same time.

7. Falah:

Success or gain–the opposite of loss [Khusra'n]. "Falah" – success, in the materialistic sense, is measured in terms of wealth, prosperity, and the maximization of power and pleasure in this world, irrespective of the fact from where and how one gets it. The person who has none of these gains is considered "loser", poor and included in the "have-nots". But in the estimation of our Creator and Sustainer, it has no value if he gets all these material gains through wrongful, dishonest and oppressive means. He will cut a sorry figure when he will be put to account for all these ill -gotten gains on the Day of Judgment. However, one who earns this world with rightful honest means and used it in the way ordained by His Lord, he/she will have "Falah", the success in both the worlds. Thus the truthful success is the success in the world Hereafter and a man should live on earth to get the "Falah" [success] in the life Hereafter, even he/she may be the loser or a pauper on this earth. The real Success is the success in the life Hereafter.

8. Fasad:

Transgression – the apposite of "Islaah" - "peace" and harmony. Allah abhors "Fasad" in human abode. "Fasad" is the direct outcome of the life style that humans observe on this earth in denying the authority of their Lord, feeling not accountable to Him for their actions and deeds on earth and denying the system of life that He recommends through His appointed messengers to follow while living on earth. "Fasad" only ends in chaos, bloodshed and disorder, making the human life and his abode insecure, fill it with injustices and all kinds of discrimination and arrogance as we see around us today and through ages. "Fasad" can be removed only by establishing His authority and His Deen-Al-Islam on earth in every walk of life. Without that human society will never experience justice, peace and security on earth.

9. "Free":

Nothing is "free" from Allah. All is conditional. You first fulfill your obligations to Allah, He will then fulfill His promises to humans except Rizq [the provision] that will be available to all, including those who negate or disobey Him. However, all must carry/meet two conditions:

1. Man will get to the extent he/she tries but how much? Only
2. What is allotted by Him?

10. Hadith Qudsi:
The Hadith {traditions or sayings] of Prophet Muhammad (S) which Is when narrated in the actual words of Allah as revealed to him (S). When Rasulullah (S) narrated it in his (S) own words, it is called Hadith

11. Jahiliyah:
Ignorance. People who ignore these facts that: * God is the Creator and Sustainer of this cosmos including humans; * they are not the masters but trustees of what He has created and entrusted in their hands; and * they are not accountable to Him for the manner they are living on this earth and using His trusts in their hands as per their free will and not in the way He ordained through His appointed messengers, they are ignorant [Jahil] and the life pattern that they are leading will be that of Jahiliyah [ignorance], irrespective of the fact howsoever they are "educated". If one's education does not lead him/her to recognize his/her Lord, he/she is ignorant # one.

12. Maghfirah:
Praying to Allah for the pardon of one's sins;

13. Maghrib:
Islam requires from every Muslim to offer Salah five times in a day. Maghrib is one of them. The schedule of Salah is arranged as follows: 1. FAJR (before sunrise); 2. ZOHR (after midday); 3. ASR (before sunsets); 4. MAGHRIB (after sunsets] & 5. ISHA (one and 1/2 hour after sunsets to mid night)

14. Millah:
The Muslim Community as elaborated above.

15. Rabb:
Sustainer. Allah is the Sustainer of all living creatures including humans. Allah claims total loyalty and unflinching obedience from His creation [the man] as He is not only the Creator but also our Sustainer too. He provides all that man needs for his/her existence on earth.

16. Sabr & Shukr:

Endurance & Thankfulness are the two important characteristics of a Mumin. A Mumin, as elaborated in this book, is always thankful to Him for all the favors and bounties that he/she gets from Allah and shows endurance when he/she is put to test or receives sorrow, troubles and sufferings.

17. Salat–ul-Tahajjud:
The non-obligatory Salah that was obligatory for Prophet Muhammad (S) but not for the Ummah. Its timing starts from midnight and continues till dawn, before the start of FAJR prayer. This Salah is of great value in cementing human relations with Allah. A Muslim or Muslimah leaves his/her bed when the world is sleeping, offers 4 to 8 Rakaah, recites the Qur'an that he/she has memorized, prostrates before Allah and begs His pardon [Maghfirah] and Khair {good] of every thing of this world and of the next. He/she begs form Him "Ilm" [knowledge], Tawfeeq, courage, Rizq-e-Halal [honest means of living] good moral behavior, straight path and stamina to struggle in His way for the Iqamah of His Deen. The more he/she cries and begs from Him the more he/she will be closer to Him. Begging pardon from Him at these hours Allah loves it.

18. Shirk:
Making partners with Allah Who is One and only One, either in His person, authority or attributes is "Shirk". Allah abhors it very vehemently. He can pardon any sin but not "Shirk", making some one His equal or worshipping someone as "God". Our Jews and Christian brothers and sisters should asses their position as where they stand.

19. Terjumanul Qur'an:
The monthly Magazine in Urdu started by Late Maulana Maududi Merhoom, the founder President of the Islamic Movement, Jamaat-e-Islami [of India/ Pakistan/BD/Sri Lanka/Nepal] in August 1941. He died in the USA in 1979 while on visit for his treatment

20. Ummah:
The community. The Muslims are a community based on the ideology of Islam - Its fundamental Faith and Creed are as follows: Monotheism; 2. Accountability on the Day of Judgment for all actions and Deeds on earth; 3. Concept of Amanah (trust); 4. Following the life pattern of Prophet Muhammad (S) as the only model to follow on earth; 5. Destiny;

BIBLIOGRAPHY

1. AL- Qur'an

2. The Meaning of The Glorious Qur'an   Muhammad M Pickthall

3. The Message of The Qur'an   Muhammad Asad

4. Tadabbur Qur'an   Late Maulana Amin Ahsan Islahi

5. Tafhimul Qur'an   Late S. A. A. Maududi

6. Maa'reful Qur'an   Late Maulana Mufti M Shafi

7. Ahadith – Saha Sitta

8. The Provision for Akhirah
   [Zaderah]   Late Maulana Jalil Ahsan Nadvi

9. The Greatest Need of Man   Shamim A Siddiqi

10. Arabic – English Lexicon   Edward W Lane